TALES FROM THE
PHILADELPHIA PHILLIES
DUGOUT

A COLLECTION OF THE GREATEST
PHILLIES STORIES EVER TOLD

RICH WESTCOTT

SPORTS
PUBLISHING

Sports Publishing books may be purchased in bulk at special discounts for sales promotion, corporate gifts, fund-raising, or educational purposes. Special editions can also be created to specifications. For details, contact the Special Sales Department, Sports Publishing, 307 West 36th Street, 11th Floor, New York, NY 10018 or sportspubbooks@skyhorsepublishing.com.

Sports Publishing® is a registered trademark of Skyhorse Publishing, Inc.®, a Delaware corporation.

Visit our website at www.sportspubbooks.com

10 9 8 7 6 5 4 3

Library of Congress Cataloging-in-Publication Data is available on file.

ISBN: 978-1-61321-036-9

Printed in the United States of America

*To the Phillies' nearly 2,000 players, managers, coaches,
and front office people who during the 123 years of this
colorful, yet unconventional franchise have seldom
ceased to make it interesting.*

Contents

Introduction vi

Chapter 1
The Early Days—1883-1899 1

Chapter 2
A New Century Begins—1900-1919 12

Chapter 3
Hard Times—1920-1939 24

Chapter 4
The Bleak Streak Continues—1940-1949 36

Chapter 5
A Temporary Surge—1950-1959 50

Chapter 6
Disasters Reign—1960-1969 66

Chapter 7
On the Way Up—1970-1979 83

Chapter 8
Reaching the Top—1980-1989 105

Chapter 9
One Moment of Glory—1990-1999 126

Chapter 10
Back in the Race Again—2000-2005 149

Chapter 11
The Best Era in Phillies History—2005-2011 170

Chapter 12
The Last Word—Views from the Press Box 183

About the Author 195

Introduction

In the 129 years of the Philadelphia Phillies, there is one unavoidable description of the franchise. It was often last, but seldom dull.

This is a club, after all, that had a lefthanded catcher named Jack Clements. Bill Hulen was a shortstop. He was also lefthanded. The Phils had a pitcher who was aptly nicknamed "Boom Boom" Beck. Another hurler bore the nickname of "Losing Pitcher" Mulcahy. After hitting over .300 in four straight seasons, outfielder Johnny Moore was sold to the highest bidder—a minor league team.

Third baseman Hans Lobert once raced a horse around the bases. First baseman Eddie Waitkus was shot by a crazed admirer. Mike Schmidt tried to disguise himself by wearing a wig onto the field. John Kruk rebelled when a woman called him an "athlete." One time Scott Rolen was forced to wear women's clothes when he left the ballpark. And Ryan Howard once claimed the he first knew he was an exceptional power hitter when his mother told him when he was about eight years old..

Darren Daulton said that the 1993 pennant-winning team was made up of "gypsies, tramps, and thieves." Reliever Tug McGraw called one of his favorite pitches "The Peggy Lee — —Is that all there is?" Jim Konstanty, another relief pitcher, trained with an undertaker. Richie Ashburn once hit the same woman twice with foul balls during the same at-bat.

"I'm 49 and I want to live to be 50," said manager Eddie Sawyer upon resigning after one game in 1960. "Even Napoleon had his Watergate," insisted manager Danny Ozark after a particularly difficult losing stretch. "It's better living off the fleas than have them living off you," affirmed ex-pitcher Grover

Cleveland Alexander when questioned about his post-retirement job at a flea circus. When asked how he liked playing on Astroturf, Dick Allen replied, "If a horse can't eat it, I don't want to play on it."

The Phillies, the oldest, continuous, one name, one city franchise in professional sports, surely have suffered more indignities than most other teams. No club ever finished in last place 31 times, as the Phils have. Who else ever lost 23 games in a row, or blew a pennant after holding a six and one-half game lead with 12 games left to play? And what team hit .315 for the season, but lost 102 games while finishing 40 games out of first place?

But look at it this way: The Phillies have become one of the best and most exciting teams in baseball. Between 2007 and 2011 they won five division titles and went to two World Series, one of which they won. That was only the second time (the first was in 1980) that the Phils have ever won the Fall Classic, although they had previously appeared in ones in 1915, 1950, 1983, and 1993.

Ah, but amid all the highs and the lows, the pranks and the putdowns, the laughter and the tears resides a lovable franchise that has seldom ceased to be interesting. The Phillies might be one of the most colorful franchises ever to emerge from a clubhouse. No drab, corporate drones are they. No, indeed. This is a franchise that could never come off an assembly line. It has its own individual mold, and if that mold was ever broken, there would be no way to duplicate it.

How could you possibly duplicate a team that had the 1950 Whiz Kids? Or the 1980 and 2008 World Series winners? Or Ed Delahanty, Grover Cleveland Alexander, Chuck Klein, Robin Roberts, Richie Ashburn, Jim Bunning, Mike Schmidt, or Steve Carlton—Hall of Famers, one and all? Or Pete Rose who should be one, too? And what could be any better than Dick Sisler's home run in 1950, Dick Allen's gargantuan clouts, Rick Wise's two-homer no-hitter, Tug McGraw's relief, Garry Maddox's defense, John Kruk's quips, Jim Eisenreich's heroic comeback, Rico Brogna's glove, Bobby Abreu's consistency, or having the three best players at their positions in club history—Howard, Chase Utley, and Jimmy Rollins—all on the same team?

And along with all the stars and superstars, the Phillies have had no shortage of entertaining characters. Some of the ones you'll meet in this book include Tim McCarver, Bob Uecker, Russ Meyer, Jeff Stone, Larry Andersen, and Jay Johnstone. All at one time or another wore the colors of the Phillies. So did world-famous evangelist Billy Sunday, NFL Pro Football Hall of Fame coach Earle (Greasy) Neale, and a guy who did some managing named Charles Dillon (Casey) Stengel.

We also squeezed in a few stories involving the media. Broadcasters and writers, a species that in some cases has reached legendary heights in Philadelphia—and that is not merely a statement describing the genius of their vocabulary—often rubbed elbows with the world of the abnormal. Some of their experiences are told here.

Many of the stories in *Tales from the Phillies Dugout* are intended to be humorous. Conveying a concentrated dose of levity is, after all, the primary focus of this book. But some stories are serious. Some are even tragic. All in all, though, this is a book about a very special franchise, its abundance of noteworthy—and often colorful—individuals, and the significant and sometimes trivial events with which they've been connected.

—RICH WESTCOTT

Chapter 1

The Early Days

1883-1899

Reaching Out

The first owner of the Phillies was a left-handed former second baseman who was born in England and who was the first professional baseball player. His name was Al Reach, and if that name sounds familiar, it's because it appeared on sporting goods, including American League baseballs, for many decades.

In 1863, Reach was paid the unfathomable sum of $1,000 for suiting up with the Athletics, an independent team in Philadelphia. The money was good for that time, but it fell a bit short of the sums Reach earned later in his flourishing sporting goods business.

Aside from making Reach wealthy, the sporting goods business was also responsible for providing the old second sacker (Ben Shibe, the future owner of the American League's Philadelphia Athletics, was Reach's partner in the business) with the means to launch a National League baseball team in Philadelphia called the Phillies. The team, having been formed to take the place of the defrocked Worcester Brown Stockings franchise, came into existence in 1883.

Actually, the Phillies crept into existence. Their entry into the big time came more like a whimper than a whirlwind. What else would you call a team that surged through its maiden season with a 17-81 record?

The Phillies, however, did set themselves up for one particular distinction. With the team having emerged from its cocoon 123 years ago, the name *Phillies* ranks as the oldest continuous nickname in American professional sports.

Which Flying Things?

The Phillies' first manager was a likeable chap with an assortment of playing and managing experience in professional baseball. His playing days dated back to 1871, and his managerial career started five years later.

The man's name was Bob Ferguson. Nothing unusual about that. But he carried the nickname of "Death to Flying Things."

Why was old Death to Flying Things called Death to Flying Things? There are several theories. One said that when he played— usually in the infield—he caught everything that was hit his way. That's an arguable position since our boy DTFT made more than 600 errors in 14 professional seasons. In his one Phillies season alone he amassed 88 miscues.

Another explanation claimed that Ferguson had the admirable ability of being able to kill all bugs that got near him. Perhaps that's a more plausible theory.

Take your pick. Whatever the answer, DTFT's career as the Phillies first skipper ended abruptly. He was fired after his team got off to a 4-13 start, although he remained as the team's regular second baseman throughout the season. Fergy's replacement, third baseman-outfielder-pitcher Blondie Purcell, guided the club to a 13-68 record the rest of the way.

A Record of Futility

The Phillies—make that every team in the major leagues—have championed a heaping measure of futility over the years. None, however, can match that of pitcher John Coleman, a right-hander who began his six-year big league career with the 1883 Phils.

As the Phillies' main hurler that first year, Coleman worked in 65 games, covering 538.1 innings. But wait, there's more. He gave up a league-leading 809 hits. Even more gruesome, Coleman's record was a super-sickly 12-48. No one in major league history has ever given up more hits, lost more games, or undoubtedly suffered a greater dose of indignity than the unfortunate Mr. Coleman.

No Wizard

For a second dose of futility, try this: In 1884, the Phillies had a new third baseman. His name was Joe Mulvey, and he spent six seasons manning the club's hot corner.

The term *manning* is used loosely. That's because Mulvey committed the staggering total of 135 errors in his first two seasons. He kicked away 73 balls the first year, then improved to 62 the second year. During his 12-year career, Mulvey collected 479 miscues in 987 games. Obviously, no wizard was Joe.

Left-Wingers

It is an unwritten rule in baseball that left-handers don't catch. And they don't play shortstop, either. Leave it to the Phillies to break the mold.

Between 1885 and 1897, the team's regular catcher was that eminent southpaw, Jack Clements. Jack worked behind the plate while wearing a right-handed catcher's mitt. Only two other backstops have caught more games for the Phils than Clements.

Not surprisingly, Clements also caught more games (1,073) than any left-handed catcher in baseball history during a 17-year

career in the big leagues. He was said to be the first catcher ever to
wear a chest protector.

Another lefty was Billy Hulen, the Phillies' regular shortstop in
1896. Hulen played in 73 games at shortstop, the highest total ever
achieved by a left-hander at that position.

The Wright Stuff

Maybe the impression given by now is that the Phillies were a
sorry bunch of incompetents not suitable for prime-time baseball.
That may have been true at the outset, but the Phils' fortunes
began to change when Harry Wright became the team's manager in
1884.

Wright's tombstone in a Philadelphia cemetery labels him "The
Father of Professional Baseball." That epitaph rings true, given the
fact that Harry was the pilot of the undefeated 1869 Cincinnati
Red Stockings, baseball's first professional team. Wright also gave
the world flannel uniforms with knickered pantlegs and colored
stockings.

Harry built the Phillies into a contending team while holding
the reins through the 1893 season. One of his—and the Phillies'—
most unusual seasons came in 1890 when Wright and three others,
including owner Al Reach, all served as managers of the team. An
eye ailment causing temporary blindness forced Wright to the
sidelines, paving the way for the others to become substitute
skippers.

No pushover, Wright, the second winningest manager in
Phillies history (behind Gene Mauch), once fined Ed Delahanty
after the slugger ignored a bunt sign. It mattered little to Wright
that Big Ed hit a home run on the pitch.

Harry was also not fond of the enthusiasm of some coaches. "I
don't approve of noisy coaches," he said. "If the Philadelphias can't
win without howling themselves hoarse, then I don't want to win
at all. This bellowing from the coaching lines isn't baseball."

Manager Harry Wright was no fan of noisy coaches.
Photo provided by National Baseball Hall of Fame Library, Cooperstown, New York

A Legitimate Beef

Not all Phillies managers have been gems like Harry Wright. Over the years, the club has had its share of bumblers who gave new meaning to the word *incompetent*. The Phils also have been richly endowed with skippers who strayed from the norm.

Arthur Irvin, a fine shortstop as a player, piloted the club in 1894-1895. Some years later, Irvin drowned when he apparently jumped from a ship in the Atlantic Ocean following the allegation that he was a bigamist.

Another "unusual" 19th-century pilot was George Stallings, a medical doctor during the offseason, but an abusive demon during the spring and summer. Stallings, later the skipper of the "Miracle Braves" in 1914, managed the Phillies in 1897 and part of 1898.

Stallings was such a nasty buzzard that the players made no attempt to hide their hatred of him. Their animosity reached the boiling point early in 1898 when a group of players led by outfielder Dick Cooley told Phillies ownership that they would no longer play for Stallings.

"We are fed up with the way Stallings has been riding us and decided we had enough of him and would regard him as our manager no longer," a statement from the players said. "For weeks, he has been handling us like cattle. We may not be the best team in the league, but we don't intend to put up with Stallings's tactics."

Soon afterward, Stallings was ushered—or was it booted?—out the door. As far as the players were concerned, justice had been served.

Preacher Man

Any student of religion can identify Billy Sunday. For the uninformed, he was a world-famous evangelist who traveled the country during the late 1800s and up to the 1930s, spreading the gospel to crowds numbering as high as 100,000. Sunday was in his day what the fictional Elmer Gantry and the real-life Billy Graham were in theirs.

But there was one critical difference. Sunday was a reformed baseball player who spent parts of eight seasons in the big leagues. His final games in 1890 were spent with the Phillies.

As the story goes, Sunday, as did most of the players of his era, liked to tilt the mug with a fair degree of regularity. One night, having tilted it a bit too often, the speedy outfielder sat on a curb and pledged to turn his life around. Eventually, he quit baseball and became a preacher.

The appropriately named Sunday, however, never lost his love for baseball. Often, he made references to the sport in his sermons. And on some occasions, he would use his baseball background to make a dramatic grand entry onto a stage.

Picture this: Thousands of people cramming an outdoor tent or hall; women wearing big, floppy hats and flowing dresses and men in immaculately pressed suits, ties, and shirts with stiff collars; flowers and ornate decor filling the stage. The hushed crowd anxiously awaits Sunday's arrival.

And then the reverend is introduced. From out of the wings he appears. He sprints across the stage, and—can you believe this?—slides into the pulpit. Whether safe or out, he has already captured the attention of his audience. What a way to launch a sermon!

Some Kind of Outfield

During the first five years of the 1890s, the Phillies had an outfield that may never again be paralleled. All three fly catchers were future members of the Hall of Fame.

Ed Delahanty, Billy Hamilton, and Sam Thompson composed this star-spangled trio. Incredibly, all three hit more than .400 during the 1894 season. Delahanty and Thompson checked in with .407 marks, while Hamilton finished the season at .404. And if that wasn't enough, reserve outfielder Tuck Turner smacked the old apple at a lofty .416.

Thompson won a pair of home run crowns with the Phillies while batting .331 for his career. Hamilton—"Sliding Billy," as he was called—was not only baseball's first great base-stealer and a onetime batting champion, but he also set a still-standing major league record in 1894 with 192 runs scored. Delahanty rapped out a .346 career average, fourth highest in baseball history.

Not Good Enough

Had it not been for an incompetent scouting report, the great Honus Wagner might have worn the colors of the Phillies instead of the Pittsburgh Pirates.

In the mid-1890s, the Phillies dispatched injured pitcher Con Lucid to New Jersey, where he was ordered to scout Wagner, who was playing for Patterson in a game against Richmond. The Phillies had heard glowing reports about Wagner and hoped to sign him.

Lucid, however, a seldom-used pitcher with obvious defects as a scout, was more enamored with Richmond shortstop Norman (Kid) Elberfeld.

"He fields like a demon," Lucid said. "I believe the boy will go far. You can't go wrong investing in him."

As for Wagner, Lucid had this to report: "He can hit, but he's too clumsy for the National League."

Elberfeld became an above-average shortstop with a 14-year big league career. But the Phillies dumped him after one year. Wagner, of course, wound up in the Hall of Fame.

Splendid Swatter

Ed Delahanty was arguably the greatest hitter in Phillies history. And why wouldn't he have been? The guy hit above .400 three times with the Phils, including .410 in 1899 when he won the National League batting crown.

Big Ed also captured three RBI titles, two home run crowns, and three times socked more than 200 hits in a season, including a league-leading 238 in 1899.

A first and second baseman before getting paroled to the outfield, Delahanty was one of five—no, that's not a typo—brothers who performed in the major leagues. Obviously the best of the quintet, Ed was the second big leaguer to hit four home runs in one game.

That memorable feat came in 1896 with the Chicago White Stockings providing the opposition. After Delahanty's fourth homer, players crowded around the slugger as he reached home plate. Incredibly, one of those players was Chicago pitcher Adonis Terry. Although he'd surrendered four home runs to an opposing batter, Adonis was so impressed with the slugging feat that he wanted to take part in the celebration. Terry shook Delahanty's hand and complimented him as he crossed the plate.

By the way, the Phillies lost 9-8. As for recognition of Big Ed's achievement? He was rewarded with four boxes of chewing gum.

Big Ed often got upset when writers incorrectly spelled his name.

"I don't think it's fair that a man who has won fame as a swatter of shots and benders should have his name misspelled," Delahanty complained.

Delahanty's life ended tragically in 1903, one and one-half years after he'd jumped to the new American League and won a batting title in his first season with the Washington Senators. A heavy drinker throughout much of his career, Delahanty was on a train on the Canadian side of Niagara Falls when, due to his rowdy behavior, he was put off the train by the conductor.

What happened after that has never been determined. Delahanty either jumped, fell, or was pushed off a bridge above the Niagara River and was washed over Niagara Falls. One week later, his mangled body was found at the bottom of the falls.

Cheapskates and Softies

There have been times over the years when it might be said that Phillies ownership was a tad cheap. Such was the case in the mid-1890s when Al Reach and his partner, Col. John Rogers, tried to cut a few corners.

At least, the way the players described it, the Phils' bigwigs made them stay in cheap hotels, travel on crummy rail lines, and—hold on to your seats—dress at the ballpark instead of putting on their battle garb in their hotel rooms and getting transported to the field in horse-drawn carriages.

After hitting four home runs in one game, Ed Delahanty was rewarded with four boxes of chewing gum. *Courtesy of Rich Westcott*

The disgruntled players complained long and loud. Finally, Rogers had heard enough.

"If you're looking for a soft job," he shouted, "you should get a job in a sponge factory!"

Beating the Buzzer

From time to time, there were whispers around the National League that gave rise to the suspicion that there must be a good reason the Phillies hit so much better at home than they did on the road. No one could lay a finger on a logical explanation until one day in 1898 when a foot discovered the answer.

Cincinnati Reds infielder Tommy Corcoran was coaching at third base, kicking up dirt, and going through the usual coaching gyrations when suddenly his spikes caught on something in the ground. What have we here, thought Corcoran.

At first, Tommy figured it was a vine. But after closer inspection, he discovered an underground wire. Corcoran gave a yank, and up came a few yards of wire. Then, with time called and players from both teams crowding around, Corcoran continued tugging on the wire. He soon found himself pulling up wire in the outfield.

In those days, the Phillies' clubhouse at the then-named Philadelphia Park was on the second level in center field. And as Corcoran continued to yank, that's exactly where the wire led— right into the Phillies' clubhouse.

At the end of the wire, the curious Corcoran found reserve catcher Morgan Murphy sitting behind an open window. He had a telegraph instrument beside him and a pair of strong opera glasses in his hand.

You can guess what Murph was doing. He, of course, was picking up the opposing catcher's signals and then with the aid of the telegraph instrument, relaying them through the wire to the Phillies' third base coaching box. There a buried buzzer that was connected to the wire would vibrate under the coach's foot. One buzz signaled a fastball, two a curve, and three a change of pace. Having determined the upcoming pitch, the coach would then relay the information to the batter.

Corcoran's discovery let the cat out of the bag. The scheme was over. So was the Phillies' home-field advantage.

Chapter 2

A New Century Begins

1900-1919

Upward Mobility

By the start of the 20th century, the Phillies had become a respectable member of the National League. During the decade of the 1890s, the club had finished in third place three times and in fourth on five occasions.

The formation of the American League in 1901 hurt the Phillies badly with the loss of future Hall of Famers Ed Delahanty, Nap Lajoie, and Elmer Flick. But after two seventh-place finishes, one eighth-place finish, and the Phils' first 100-loss season, the team eventually bounced back, winning its first pennant in 1915. Although it lost in five games in the World Series to the Boston Red Sox, that club had its own future Hall of Famer, pitcher Grover Cleveland Alexander. He had been purchased from the minor league team at Syracuse for the bargain-basement sum of $750.

As was often the case with the Phillies, managers came and went about as regularly as parades on the Fourth of July. Six managers piloted the team between 1900 and 1915. The group included a former ticket taker (Billy Shettsline), a future umpire (Chief Zimmer), the owner of baseball's highest batting average (Hugh Duffy), a hot-tempered Irishman (Billy Murray), an offseason vaudeville singer (Red Dooin), and the man who would become the skipper of the 1919 Cincinnati Reds (Pat Moran).

Under their reigns during the first 16 years of the new century, the Phillies finished in every place in the standings at least once.

In 1916, the Phillies also scratched out another significant number. This one involved center fielder Dode Paskert. An advertisement placed on the right-center field wall at Baker Bowl by a bug-snaring company proclaimed, "Dode Paskert caught 209 flies last season. Our fly catcher caught 1,237,345."

Down with the Mendoza Line

We're always hearing about the "Mendoza Line." Anytime a hitter goes into a serious slump, we're told that he's threatening to fall below the dreaded Mendoza Line.

Phooey on the Mendoza Line. It's a fraud. So what if a guy named Mario Mendoza is credited with having an average so low that when anybody has the misfortune of falling below it, he immediately suffers the indignity of being associated with the former light-hitting shortstop.

Mendoza's line is .198. He hit that in 148 games in 1979. What's so bad about that?

Ever heard of a guy named Bill Hallman? He makes Mario Mendoza look like Ernie Banks. Hallman once hit .184. Now, that's a line not to be crossed.

Hallman etched his name in the barnyard while playing both second and third base for the Phillies in 1901. In 445 trips to the plate, he managed just 82 hits, none of them homers, five of them triples, and 13 of them doubles. The curious thing about such ineptitude is that for four straight seasons with the Phillies in the mid-1890s, Hallman hit over .300 each time, and in a 14-year career carried a lifetime average of .272. Hallman was traded by the Phillies in 1897, but then returned to the team early in 1901.

Maybe the trauma of coming back sabotaged his swing. Whatever the case, let's hear it for the newly named Hallman Line.

A Matter of Perspective

There was never a Phillies pitcher any better than Grover Cleveland Alexander. Matter of fact, few hurlers in all of baseball were any better than Ol' Pete.

An early Hall of Fame inductee, Alexander won 373 games during a legendary 20-year big league career. In his seven years with the Phillies, Alex won 190 games, three times winning 30 or more. While winning 94 games over a three-year period, Alexander's ERA ranged from 1.22 to 1.86. In 1915 when he led the Phillies to their first pennant, he pitched four one-hitters. That year, he won the World Series opener. And in 1916 he set an all-time record with 16 shutouts.

But the man noted for his brilliant pitching didn't have an easy life after his retirement in 1930. Alexander, who was named after a U.S. president and who was played by a future U.S. president (Ronald Reagan) in a movie about his life, lost too many decisions to the bottle. This, and other problems, made it virtually impossible for the great hurler to hold a job.

At one point in his post-playing days, one of Ol' Pete's many unflattering jobs was as a shill at a flea circus near Times Square in New York City. After being discovered in such lowly surroundings, Alex was asked by a disbeliever how he could have let himself sink to such a dismal level.

"It's better living off the fleas," Alexander somberly replied, "than having them living off you."

◆ ◆ ◆

No doubt about it, Alexander was a workhorse. He pitched in more than 300 innings in nine different seasons, including all

In one of his jobs, Grover Cleveland Alexander (right) earned a living by working at a flea circus.
Courtesy of Rich Westcott

seven years with the Phillies. On occasion, he exceeded the call of duty.

Such was the case in 1916 at a doubleheader on a getaway day in Philadelphia. Alexander had already won the first game against the Cincinnati Reds when Phils manager Pat Moran came to him with a special request.

"I have to ask you to pitch the second game, too," Moran said. "We only have a little more than an hour to catch the train. Get it over fast."

Ever the dutiful player, the likeable Alex complied. He pitched a shutout. The game was played in 58 minutes.

◆ ◆ ◆

Alexander had magnificent control. During his entire career, he walked just 951 batters in 5,190 innings.

So good was Ol' Pete's control that the noted sportswriter Grantland Rice once wrote: "He could pitch into a tin can."

Silent Tight

Although he played with the Phillies for 10 years starting in 1903, John Titus was the kind of guy who was so quiet that hardly anybody ever knew he was around. That's why he was called "Silent John."

Titus was also called "Tight Pants" for obvious reasons. Moreover, the outfielder always went to bat with a toothpick in his mouth. But his most noticeable trait was his reluctance to emit sounds.

"He doesn't even make any noise when he spits," infielder Kid Gleason observed.

No More Secrets

There was no mystery regarding how Harry Coveleski got the nickname "Giant Killer." As a rookie in 1908, the Phillies pitcher beat the New York Giants three times in seven days late in the season, knocking John McGraw's club out of a chance to win outright the National League pennant, instead forcing the Giants into a playoff, which they lost to the Chicago Cubs.

Brought up from the minors just a few weeks earlier, Coveleski in his first start had paid no attention to a runner taking a big lead at first base. Naturally, the runner stole second. Naturally, Phillies manager Bill Murray was furious.

"Why didn't you hold that runner on base?" Murray fumed after the inning was over.

"I didn't know he was there," responded the raw rookie.

After the game, Murray held a meeting with Coveleski, catcher Red Dooin, and the four infielders.

Addressing first baseman Kitty Bransfield, Murray said angrily, "Kitty, did you know there was a runner on first and not tell Covey?"

Bransfield pleaded guilty. Murray then asked the three other infielders and Dooin the same question. Each said he knew the runner was at first, but had not told Coveleski.

Finally, feigning extreme aggravation, Murray pounded his fist on the table and screamed, "From now on, we'll have no further secrets on this club. Whenever a runner gets to base on Harry, I want you men to tell him. Do you all understand?"

The Fightin' Live Wires

Of all the people who have served as president of the Phillies, Horace Fogel surely ranked as one of the strangest. He had, after all, been a sportswriter at a Philadelphia newspaper. How many sportswriters ever ascended to such a lofty status?

Fogel had briefly managed the 1902 New York Giants, but was promptly sent back to the newspaper business after he tried to convert Christy Mathewson into a first baseman. Once Horace took over the Phillies (mostly, of course, with other people's money), he quickly exhibited his promotional genius. One of his biggies was to have a couple married in a lion's cage on the pitcher's mound with the lion serving as a witness.

That didn't work out, but Horace had other ideas. One was to change the name of the Phillies to Live Wires.

"The word *Phillies* is too trite," he said. "It has come to mean a comfortable lackadaisicalness [an ex-sportswriter said that?], the fourth-place groove. And Quakers [a name the Phillies were sometimes called] stands for peaceful people who will dodge a fight. We're not going to be that way. We're going to get into fights."

So Fogel urged people to call the team the Live Wires. He had trinkets made showing wires dangling from an eagle. On opening day in 1910, unable to get an eagle, he borrowed 100 pigeons, had admission tickets strapped to their legs, and sent them aloft.

The name, however, never stuck.

Alas, Fogel's baseball career came to an unhappy end. He was banned from baseball by a jury of other team owners after he made comments that implied that the 1912 National League pennant race was fixed. Presumably, Horace had no comment.

Beaten by a Horse

One of the fastest players of his era was John (Hans) Lobert, a veteran of 14 big league seasons, four of them as the Phillies' third baseman. How fast was Hans? He was once clocked circling the bases in 13.8 seconds, a superb time even in the present era of speedsters.

Hans was so fast, in fact, that he once raced a horse around the bases. The match occurred in 1913 while Lobert—often called "Honus" because of his close resemblance to the great Honus Wagner—was barnstorming in California with a team assembled by New York Giants manager John McGraw.

Then playing with the Phillies, Lobert—a future Phillies manager—was supposed to run inside the base paths and the horse would run outside the paths. With numerous bets having been placed, Hans took an early lead, but after rounding second, the horse cut too close to him, causing the Phillies infielder to break stride. The horse passed Lobert between third and home, winning the race by a nose. Hans protested, saying the horse had broken the rules, but the outcome stood.

He Became a What?

In the early days of the 20th-century Phillies, it's unlikely that any player had a hotter temper than outfielder Sherry Magee. A hard-hitting left fielder and highly adept base-stealer, Magee ignited numerous sparks during his 11 years with the Phillies.

Once, he dropped a bag full of water out of a hotel window onto the head of pitcher Eppa Rixey. Another time, Magee was feuding with fellow outfielder Dode Paskert. One day Paskert hit a home run, and as he rounded the bases, he was loudly booed from the stands by Magee's two sons. When Dode reached the dugout, he headed straight for Magee, and the two engaged in a lively display of fisticuffs.

Magee's most notorious explosion occurred in a game in 1911 after he was called out on strikes by umpire Bill Finneran. Having been thrown out of the game the previous day, Sherry was in no mood for haggling. Instead, he hauled off and socked Finneran squarely on the jaw. It was a clean KO, and the umpire thudded to the ground.

For demonstrating his boxing prowess, Magee was fined $200 and suspended for the rest of the season. The suspension was later reduced to 36 days.

The story, however, had a stunning postscript. Several years later, after his retirement in 1919, Magee became a big league umpire.

Homeboy

Gavvy Cravath was not only one of the top power hitters in Phillies history, but he was also one of the major leagues' first big sluggers of the 20th century. The Phils outfielder won six National League home run crowns over a seven-year period between 1913 and 1919.

Cravath's total of 24 home runs in 1915 was the highest single-season mark in the major leagues in the 20th century until Babe Ruth passed it with 29 homers in 1919. A right-handed batter,

Cravath had won the NL's home run crown in 1914 with 19 dingers. Amazingly, all 19 homers were hit at Baker Bowl, the Phillies' home ballpark.

Spring Draining

There was a time long, long ago when spring training was not the fun-filled, luxurious interlude it has become. The annual preseason ritual was a bare-bones, loathsome abomination that was pure, unadulterated drudgery.

For the Phillies, 1915 exemplified that unpopular time of the year. That season the team convened in St. Petersburg, Florida under new manager Pat Moran at an uninviting field called Coffee Pot Park. Perhaps the grounds were covered with grounds.

There was one cold shower for all. The rickety wooden park held about 500. Moran made the players walk the two miles from their hotel in downtown St. Pete to the field. When he discovered that pitchers Joe Oeschger and Stan Baumgartner were riding bicycles instead of walking, he made them walk an extra mile each day.

Moran held workouts in the morning and afternoon. In between, some players fished in the bayou behind the field or went to an adjacent grove to pick oranges. Some of them ate the terrible food provided for lunch. Fried fish with the heads still in place were often served. Other times, roast beef was the fare of the day. The beef was so tough that one day, Grover Cleveland Alexander nailed a slab to his shoe, using it as a sole. It may have been his way of saying that the players had a lot to beef about.

Making Due with Less

"This is your bread and butter as well as mine," Pat Moran would tell his players, trying to prod them to victory in his regular pregame speeches. Of course, in those days the bread was stale and the butter was rancid.

New manager Pat Moran made players walk two miles to their spring training field. *Photo provided by National Baseball Hall of Fame Library, Cooperstown, New York*

Although players' salaries then were less than a player gets for a single at-bat today, the other conditions were no better. Players rode to the ballparks in trolleys. They traveled in hot Pullman cars, a block of ice parked above the open transom in the hope that it would deflect cool air. Players stayed in less than first-class hotels. And their meal money was $2.50 a day.

In many respects, the Phillies' first encounter with a World Series was a disaster. Grover Cleveland Alexander pitched the Phils to victory in the opener, but a sore arm kept him from taking the mound again during the Series.

The Phillies wound up losing four straight games. It didn't help that miserly Phillies owner William Baker installed temporary seats in center field to pad the crowd and hence his own bank account. The seats sliced a big piece out of the outfield and made for cheap home runs. That condition came back to bite Baker in the back when Harry Hooper hit two homers into the center field seats in the fifth game. The second, the first walkoff dinger in World Series history, gave the Boston Red Sox the Series victory in five games.

The Series did, however, attract a special visitor. In the second game played at Philadelphia's Baker Bowl, President Woodrow Wilson became the first sitting U.S. chief executive to attend a World Series game. Hard as this may be to believe, Wilson paid for his own ticket and his own scorecard.

Let's Party

Although the Phillies lost the 1915 World Series in five games to the Boston Red Sox, the losers were in no mood to slink quietly out of the clubhouse following the final game.

No indeed, a celebration was in order.

Beer kegs were rolled into the Baker Bowl clubhouse, and soon the party was underway. The Phillies' first pennant winners (and the only ones during the club's first 67 years) drank their proverbial knickers off. The party ran well into the night. As the evening progressed, players passed out and had to be carried from the clubhouse.

Catcher Bill (Reindeer Bill) Killefer won the party boy of the year award. Carted to a nearby station and packed onto a train that would carry him home to Michigan, "Paw Paw," as he was also known, didn't awake until he was passing through Altoona.

Hopefully, he didn't come to while the train was going around the city's famous horseshoe curve.

The Unnatural

Nobody ever mistook Phillies owner William Baker for Albert Einstein. Nobody ever mistook Baker for Buster Einstein, either. Baker was something less than a genius. Especially when it came to running a baseball team.

In 1918, the Phillies finished in sixth place, the result mainly of Baker's trading Alexander for two players (Mike Prendergast and Pickles Dillhoefer) who subsequently appeared in a combined total of 46 Phillies games before dropping by the wayside. At the end of the season, manager Pat Moran, who in the three previous years had guided the Phillies to a pennant and two second-place finishes, was fired. He was replaced by former Philadelphia Athletics pitcher Jack Coombs.

"I know you will all commend me on my choice," Baker told the press. "Jack is a managerial natural."

Coombs lasted 62 games. He compiled an 18-44 record as the Phillies headed for three straight last-place finishes. Although he went on to a highly successful career as a college baseball coach, most notably at Duke University, Coombs never managed in the majors again.

Chapter 3

Hard Times

1920-1939

Hey Buddy, Can You Spare Anything?

Financial shortages were a regular problem with the Phillies of the 1920s and 1930s. Club president William Baker and later chief executive Gerry Nugent both were plagued by money problems, mainly because the Phillies were badder than bad, played in a decrepit ballpark, and barely drew enough people to fill a Pullman car.

So bad were the Phillies' finances that Baker once kept slugger Cy Williams home from a season-ending road trip so that Williams couldn't pass Babe Ruth's mark of 41 home runs for the season. Another time, Baker added 12 feet of screen to the 40-foot-high right field wall to thwart the home run production of his own Chuck Klein, thereby reducing the big basher's certain higher salary demands.

"Home runs have become too cheap at the Philadelphia park," Baker alibied. The statement was a sad commentary on the Phillies' situation.

At various times in the 1930s, Nugent traded away star players such as Dick Bartell, Chuck Klein, Bucky Walters, Dolph Camilli, Claude Passeau, and Kirby Higbe, always getting players and a big chunk of cash in return. Walters and Camilli became National League Most Valuable Players for other teams, and Passeau pitched his team to a World Series.

In one instance, money was so tight that Nugent, who, a writer once said, "makes pennants in Philadelphia, but doesn't fly them there," was forced to sell the office furniture to help cover the team's expenses for spring training. Another time, he used his own meager salary to pay off a debt.

The Phillies were so financially challenged that at spring training one year, Higbe said that the hotel rooms "were so small you had to go out into the hall to change your mind. When you shaved," he added, "you had to dust the mirror off with your eyelashes."

Between 1919 and 1947, the Phillies set an all-time record for futility. How bad were they? In those 29 years, the club finished in eighth place 17 times, including five times in a row when they lost more than 100 games in each season. There were also eight seventh-place finishes, and only once did the team finish in the first division (fourth in 1932).

What a Group

Although they both finished deep in the National League cellar, the 1920 and 1921 Phillies were not total losers. The rosters of each team had some special personalities.

Among those who played with one or both teams were pitcher Lee Meadows, the first major league player to wear glasses on the field; outfielder Emil (Irish) Meusel, whose more prominent brother Bob was a New York Yankees star; Gene Paulette, a first baseman who was banned for life from baseball for associating with gamblers; and pitcher Stan Baumgartner, who, after his playing days ended, covered the Phillies as a writer with *The Philadelphia*

Inquirer (often—heaven forbid—wearing his Phillies cap in the press box).

Another hurler, Jimmy Ring, would try to avoid assignments on the mound by showing up at the ballpark with iodine painted over the fingers of his throwing hand, saying he had suffered cuts and couldn't pitch. Yet another moundsman, Flint Rhem, once disappeared for three days, only to return with the story that he'd been kidnapped.

"He looked awful hungover to me," said Dick Bartell.

Two other notables were Earle (Greasy) Neale and Casey Stengel. Neale went on to a glittering career as a college and pro football coach, earning his way into the Pro Football Hall of Fame after guiding the Philadelphia Eagles to NFL championships in 1948 and 1949. Stengel, much later a manager of some note, was so happy when the Phillies traded him in 1921 that he raced half-dressed from the clubhouse during a rain delay and circled the bases, sliding into each base, and then covered with mud, dived into home plate.

"I've just been traded to the Giants," he roared gleefully.

Heckler in Disguise

It was often said that the Phillies of the 1920s and 1930s had the worst fans in baseball. Perhaps such a trait was justifiable. The Phils also had the worst team in baseball.

Philadelphia may have been the birthplace of boobirds. And long before Eagles fans threw snowballs at Santa Claus, Phillies fans demonstrated their annoyance by throwing seat cushions onto the field at Baker Bowl.

One afternoon during batting practice, a farmer seated in the stands unleashed a tirade at the Phillies.

"I can do as good as you can, you bums," he shouted. "You can't hit. You can't do nothin'."

A Phillies player sidled over to the stands.

"You think you're so smart, you try to hit," he told the heckler.

The farmer took the bait and moved onto the field, donning a pair of spikes the team had let him borrow. He strode to the plate and promptly smacked a home run over the right field wall.

For weeks afterward, having not seen him again, the fans wondered what had happened to the homer-hitting farmer. Little did they realize that the farmer was really a noted prankster and the Phillies had gone along with the gag. The farmer was a Phillies outfielder named Casey Stengel.

The Brooklyn Phillies

Picture this: The Phillies are playing in Ebbets Field against the Brooklyn Dodgers. It's the early 1920s, and naturally, the Phils are just a step in front of a condition called disaster. And they're wearing Dodgers uniforms.

"We'd lost 11 games in a row," explained Huck Betts, a Phillies pitcher at the time. "We stopped in Brooklyn, but all our trunks had gotten lost. We had no uniforms, no nothing. So we took the field in Brooklyn's away uniforms with the Dodgers' shoes and gloves. And we beat them. Then darned if we didn't get home and lose 12 straight."

Maybe the Phillies, as they say, should've stayed in Brooklyn.

Back to the Farm

The Phillies' financial situation got so bad that even the groundskeeper was affected.

His name was Sam Payne, and his job was to maintain the playing field at Baker Bowl, despite not having much help.

The job was too much for one man. And so in desperation, Payne hired some sheep to help keep the grass trimmed. When they weren't cutting (or eating) the grass, the sheep—two ewes and a ram—resided under the left field stands.

At the time, Billy Shettsline, a ticket taker turned manager turned club president, was still an officer with the team. One day, the ponderous Shettsline—weighing in excess of 300 pounds—was wandering across the field when the ram decided to charge him.

Shettsline, running like a wounded buffalo, barely escaped the ram's wrath.

But the honeymoon was over for the sheep. A few days later, they were handed their unconditional releases.

Divine Providence

When the Phillies hired former Athletics star Stuffy McInnis as manager in 1927, owner William Baker held his perfunctory press conference to introduce his latest pigeon.

"The Phillies have turned the corner," Baker chortled.

In answer to that, one wag in the press wrote, "The Phillies may have turned the corner, but only God knows where they're going."

Mound Misery

The Phillies' dismal record hit the depths of futility in 1930. That year, the team, with five regulars hitting above .300, compiled a team batting average of .315, the third highest mark in National League history. The Phils' juggernaut was led by Chuck Klein, who hit .386 with 40 homers and 170 RBI, and Lefty O'Doul, who swatted out a .383 average.

Guess where the Phillies finished? Answer: Dead last, 40 games out of first. The Phils' record was 52-102.

"How can you finish last with such a hitting club?" manager Burt Shotton was asked.

"Have you looked at my pitching by any chance?" Shotton replied.

The heavy hitting was more than offset by a woeful pitching staff that had a 6.71 team earned run average while allowing 1,993 hits in 1,373 innings and a major league-record 1,199 runs. The average score of games at the Phils' Baker Bowl was 8-7 in favor of the opposition.

Use More Soap

In its declining years, Baker Bowl provided some high-level comedy, not only because of its decrepit condition, but because of the team that played there. It was a neck-and-neck race to determine which was worse, the ballpark or the team.

A particular laughingstock was the right field wall. At first it stood 272 feet down the line from home plate. Later, it was moved all the way back to 280. Pop flies flew over the wall for home runs with depressing regularity, and line drives that might have been homers crashed into the old tin and fell for singles or doubles. The Phillies had a standing policy that if your car windshield was broken by a batted ball as you drove down Broad Street (which ran behind the right field wall), you could come around to the front gate and get reimbursed for the damage. Such an offer may have made a sizeable contribution to the poor financial condition of the team.

In the 1920s and the early 1930s, a huge advertising sign dominated the tin, pock-marked right field wall. It said, "The Phillies use Lifebuoy." Lifebuoy was written in large letters. Below that, a fan had scribbled with a paintbrush, "And they still stink."

Now Pitching for the Phillies...

If you were a member of the Phillies in the 1920s or 1930s, it helped to have a sense of humor. What better way to get through the horrors of playing for such sickly teams?

Few had a better sense of humor than second baseman Fresco Thompson. As captain of the team, the future Brooklyn Dodgers vice president occasionally took the lineup to home plate at the start of a game.

One day, in the midst of the 1930 season, Thompson filled out the lineup card and presented it to umpire Bill Klem. In the pitcher's spot, Thompson had written, "Willoughby and others."

Shortstop was originally not Dick Bartell's position of choice.
Photo provided by National Baseball Hall of Fame Library, Cooperstown, New York

The Making of a Shortstop

What determines the position played by a major leaguer? The answer, of course, varies.

In many cases, a player's position is decided when he's a youth. Others come by their spots in the field after they've become pros.

Then there was Dick Bartell. Bartell, who spent four seasons with the Phillies, had his position decided by his father.

"I was a second baseman in high school," Bartell explained. "I wanted to be a second baseman like my dad. But the coach switched me to shortstop. I didn't want to play shortstop. So I quit the team."

Bartell came home and told his father what he'd done. An argument broke out between the elder and younger Bartell.

"Finally," Dick said, "he grabbed me by the seat of my pants, and took me back to the field. He marched me up to the coach and said, 'Here's your shortstop.'"

And that's how Bartell became one of baseball's premier shortstops and the National League starter at that position in 1933 in the first All-Star Game.

Onions for Lunch

One of the greatest hitters the Phillies ever had was a left-handed-hitting swatter who went by the name of Chuck Klein. No one in baseball had a better first six years than Klein, whose batting average ranged from .337 to .386 during that period. Between 1928 and 1933, Klein led the National League in home runs four times, in runs scored three times, and in RBI twice. And he was the NL's MVP in 1933 when he won the triple crown.

But the future Hall of Famer with the lifetime .320 batting average also had another statistic attached to his name that had nothing to do with hitting. In 1930, the Phils' right fielder threw out 44 base runners. The achievement is a still-standing major league record for an outfielder.

Klein's assist total was aided by the nearness of the right field wall to the infield. It stood just 280 feet from home plate.

"If the right fielder had eaten onions at lunch," said Red Smith, then a young Philadelphia sportswriter, "the second baseman knew it."

Chuck Klein could hit, and he wasn't bad in the field, either. *Courtesy of Rich Westcott*

Secrets of Hitting

Ethan Allen was not only one of the first major league players to hold bachelor's and master's degrees, he was also the longtime baseball coach at Yale University and the creator of All-Star Baseball, a popular board game played with disks. Allen was also a fine hitter during 13 years in the big leagues, compiling a .300 batting average.

While playing with the Phillies, Allen hit .330 in 1934, leading the National League with 42 doubles. Despite his college education, the hard-hitting outfielder had a decidedly nonacademic explanation for his solid work at the plate.

"I always felt," he said, "that when you were hitting, you could hit anybody. When you weren't hitting, you couldn't hit your Aunt Katie."

Sweet Switch

Bucky Walters broke in as a third baseman, and he stayed there through the early years of his career. As guardians of the hot corner go, however, he wouldn't quite rank near the head of the list.

Walters joined the Phillies in 1934, and that season he was the club's regular third sacker, hitting a respectable .260. But manager Jimmie Wilson had other ideas.

Wilson was also a catcher, and he could see that there was more to Walters's throwing arm than skin and bone. Wilson convinced a skeptical Walters that he would have a short career as a third baseman and that he should try pitching.

"Before I'm through with you," Wilson said, "you'll be one of the best in the game."

Jimmie turned out to be an astute judge of talent and an excellent tutor. He was also a skilled forecaster. Walters went on to become a three-time 20-game winner while being the victor 198 times during his long career. He was the National League's Most Valuable Player in 1939, winning 27 games and leading the league in complete games, earned run average, and innings pitched.

Of course, none of Walters's accomplishments was achieved with the Phillies. Bucky was traded to the Reds in 1938 for two players and the obligatory bundle of cash.

In mid-career, Hugh Mulcahy went from the ballfield to the barracks.
Courtesy of Rich Westcott

A Raw Deal

There was no better hitter on the mid-1930s Phillies than Johnny Moore. The talented outfielder with a career .307 batting average in 10 big league seasons had four straight years with the Phils when he hit well above .300, his high being .343 in 1934.

But after hitting .319 in 1937, Moore was unbelievably and unceremoniously sold to the Los Angeles Angels of the Pacific Coast League. That begs the question: How in the name of all that defies logic could a team badly in need of good players sell one of its stars to a minor league team?

"They often sold players when they needed money," Moore said. "They needed money again this time, so they sold me to Los Angeles. I heard that Brooklyn was interested in me, but I guess Los Angeles offered more money."

As a sad postscript to this incredible saga, Moore stayed in Los Angeles for the next eight years. Although he won one PCL batting title, he never returned to the big leagues except to make a token appearance in 1945 with the Chicago Cubs.

Losing Pitcher

Actually, Hugh Mulcahy was a pretty good pitcher. His record just made it seem otherwise. His nickname didn't help, either.

On a franchise that has had pitchers with nicknames such as Phenomenal (John Smith), Boom Boom (Walter Beck), Weeping Willie (Claude Willoughby), Fidgety Phil (Phil Collins), Shucks (Hub Pruett), and Wild Thing (Mitch Williams), Losing Pitcher may be the most unflattering. Poor Hugh came by the name naturally.

Over four seasons between 1937 and 1940, Mulcahy lost a total of 76 games, including 20 one year and 22 another. To be sure, many of those defeats could be charged to the ineptitude of Mulcahy's teammates. The Phillies, after all, lost more than 100 games three times and 92 once during Hugh's four-year run.

Mulcahy, however, was no loser when it came to serving his country. Hugh was the first major league player inducted into the military in World War II. He served nearly five years, which, as happened to many other players, effectively finished him as a player.

Chapter 4

The Bleak Streak Continues

1940-1949

Astute Observer

A bout as bleak a time as there was in Phillies history occurred from the late 1930s until the mid-1940s. At no time were the Phillies more pathetic.

Between 1938 and 1942, the Phils lost more than 100 games five straight times. That's a record that no team ever topped. And between 1936 and 1945, the Phillies lost 100 or more games seven times while finishing in last place eight times and in seventh twice. Since then, the Phillies have lost 100 or more games in a season only once (1961).

The franchise hit an all-time low in 1941 when it lost 111 games, a club record. The following year, it took a powder 109 times.

At the time, the Phillies had a young second baseman named Danny Murtaugh. As a rookie in 1941, he led the National League in stolen bases with 18—they didn't run much in those days. As a future manager of considerable success, Murtaugh was already showing at a young age his astute powers of observation.

Viewing the Phils' miserable records, Murtaugh exclaimed, "When we win a few games in a row, it might be cause for a congressional investigation."

New Focals Not Necessary

For some reason, the Phillies have specialized in offbeat pitchers. Over the years, legions of these unusual critters have bounced off the walls and onto pitching mounds wherever Phillies funsters assembled.

One such hurler was a right-hander whose name nobody could pronounce. Johnny Podgajny was a painfully thin moundsman of no particular note. He was so thin that when Jimmie Wilson was managing the Chicago Cubs, the former Phillies pilot would yell, "Put him in an iron lung."

The beleaguered Podgajny also wore glasses. Once, while pitching in the minors, the manager noticed that Johnny was looking over his glasses to get the catcher's signs.

The manager suggested that Podgajny buy a pair of bifocals.

"Buy focals, nothing," Podgajny roared. "I just bought these."

Later, it was discovered that Johnny bought the new specs because he "liked the feel of them."

Unexpected Help

During his 11-year big league career, Danny Litwhiler had one particular achievement that placed him above the pack. He was the first outfielder who played 100 or more games and fielded a perfect 1.000 for the season.

That happened in 1942 while Litwhiler patrolled left field for the Phillies. He played in 151 games with nary an error. That was a bit ironic because Danny had booted 15 balls the year before. Even more ironic was that Litwhiler got a big boost from an opposing player.

Johnny Podgajny liked the glasses he already had. *Courtesy of Rich Westcott*

That happened during a game late in the season at the Polo Grounds. There had been a torrential rainstorm, and although the ground had been covered, there was still a huge puddle in left field. During the game, New York Giants slugger Johnny Mize lashed a liner to left-center. Litwhiler charged across the field in hot pursuit, but had to run right through the puddle. As he reached out trying for a shoestring catch, Litwhiler slid 20 feet across the water. The ball hit the fingertip of his glove and rolled away.

The play was ruled an error. But returning to Philadelphia that night, Litwhiler bought a newspaper and saw no error listed in the box score. The next day he got up at 5 a.m. to buy another paper. Still no error.

"I couldn't figure it out," Litwhiler said. "But 10 years later, I was at a banquet in New York, and Mel Allen came over to me. And he told me what had happened."

It seems Mize was hitting .299 at the time, and wanting to hit .300, he had run, still in uniform, up to the press box after the game to confront the official scorer.

"How the hell can you give that kid an error on a play like that?" Mize fumed.

Then, turning to Allen, the scorer said, "What do you think, Mel?"

The broadcaster said, "I think it was a hit."

"OK," said the scorekeeper, "I'll give him a hit."

And that's how Litwhiler's perfect season was preserved. Danny went on to run his errorless streak to 187 games. He made just 23 errors during the rest of his career.

Sharing the Load

Nick Etten—real name Nicholas Raymond Thomas Etten— was a good-hit, no-field first baseman whose main claim to fame was that he led the American League in home runs with 22—you read that right—in 1944 while playing with the New York Yankees.

Etten also played first base in a Phillies uniform during the 1941 and 1942 seasons. In the first of those seasons, he led the club with a .311 batting average. But fielding was never his forte. It was hardly even a word in his vocabulary.

Danny Murtaugh played alongside Etten at second base. One day, Murtaugh said, "Nick, I think there are a few balls being hit down here that you should make an attempt to reach."

Years later, Danny Litwhiler finally learned what kept his errorless streak alive. *Courtesy of Rich Westcott*

Etten gave Murtaugh a funny look, and said, "Son, they pay Ol' Nick to hit. You can't hit, so you catch all those balls, and I'll knock in the runs for both of us."

Managerial Madness

Hans Lobert had a shot at managing the Phillies twice. Both times he struck out, swinging.

A Phillies third baseman back in the dark ages of baseball, Lobert had a brief shot at managing in 1938 when he guided the Phillies to two losses at the end of the season after Jimmie Wilson had been unseated from his dugout perch. Hans wasn't offered the job the following year; it went instead to a practicing dentist who went by the name of Doc Prothro (father of former football coach Tommy Prothro).

Lobert was rewarded for his long service, however, in 1942 when the Phillies handed him the reins. Hans, who had once spent eight years as head baseball coach at West Point, wasted no time instituting changes.

With the United States at war, in spring training he had the players perform military drills that were taught by Army instructors. The players would then march onto the field at exhibition games with bats on their shoulders.

Lobert also had a phobia about opposing teams stealing his signs. To compensate, he had a different set of signs for each player. Sometimes, he would use the same sign for two different players, but they would each mean different things.

"He did it to confuse the opposition," shortstop Bobby Bragan said. "But sometimes he confused his own players."

There was no confusion in the front office. After the Phillies posted a 42-109 record while finishing 62 games out of first, Lobert was relieved of his duties.

Who's a Jerk?

Of all their dubious records, none is more dubious than the one that pertains to Phillies presidents. The team has had two chief executives who were banned for life from baseball. William Cox became number two (Horace Fogel was the first) when he was booted from the game just nine months after he'd become president of the team.

Cox headed a 30-man syndicate that had picked up the club in 1943 after it had been taken over in 1942 by the National League. Cox, who often worked out with the team, liked to meddle in the club's on-field affairs. He especially liked to barge into the clubhouse and give instructions to the players.

This, of course, infuriated new manager Bucky Harris, who had performed wonders in bringing the Phillies a small measure of respectability. Harris hated Cox. The feeling was mutual, although Cox was the one who had brought Bucky to the Phillies.

One day, Cox stormed into the locker room, shouting about his worthless players and calling them "those jerks."

"The only jerk around here," shot back Harris, "is the president of the ball club."

Ultimately, Cox fired Harris, causing a brief player revolt. But Bucky, a future Hall of Fame manager, got his revenge. In his exit press conference, Harris mentioned that Cox had bet on Phillies games. The remarks set off a firestorm. Before it was over, commissioner Kenesaw Mountain Landis had banished Cox from baseball.

War-Time Wonders

Like most other teams during World War II, the Phillies were a raggedy outfit that relied on a cast of thousands to field a team. Players, most of whom gave new meaning to the word *major leaguer*, came and went by the busload. In 1945 alone, no less than 49 players appeared on the team's roster.

At one point or another, the Phillies' roster included 16-year-old Putsy Caballero and 17-year-old Granny Hamner. It included pro basketball coach Pat Riley's father, Lee, pitcher George Hennessey, who was only available for home games because he worked as an airplane mechanic in Trenton, and a guy with the unlikely name of Turkey Tyson, not to mention unforgettables such as Hilly Flitcraft, Bitsy Mott, Moon Mullen, Apples Lapihuska, and Garton DelSavio (now, there's a baseball name!).

Even aging Hall of Famers such as Jimmie Foxx, Lloyd Waner, and Chuck Klein—all well into their 40s—got into the act. Fortunately, these old-timers never got worn out traveling to spring training. Between 1943 and 1945, the Phils warmed up for the upcoming season at such hot spots as Hershey, Pennsylvania, and twice at Wilmington, Delaware.

No Blue Jays in This Flock

When 28-year-old Bob Carpenter and his family assumed ownership of the Phillies after William Cox was kicked out of baseball, many changes were put into motion. One of the first was to try to find a new nickname for the team.

This wasn't the first time an attempt had been made to give the fumbling franchise a new nickname. Horace Fogel had tried and failed to rename the team the Live Wires. Ditto for Hans Lobert, who after becoming manager in 1942, wanted to change the name to Phils because Phillies emitted a negative image.

Carpenter went about the task differently. He held a contest. There were 5,064 entries. The winning entry was Blue Jays.

The team quickly moved to make the change. It changed its logo, its stationery, it even put Blue Jays on its caps. But, alas, no one really cared. An exception was the student body at Johns Hopkins University in Baltimore, where the teams had been carrying the nickname Blue Jays for 68 years.

The students passed a resolution. Carpenter's use of the name Blue Jays, the resolution said, "is a reprehensible act which brings disgrace and dishonor to the good name of Johns Hopkins University."

The Phillies never officially adopted the name. After carrying it as a secondary nickname for several years, it quietly disappeared, never again to fly until it landed in Toronto, where, irony of ironies, the Phillies once ran a minor league team.

Stop the Music

Speaking of flakes, which is not hard to do when you're talking about the Phillies, Jimmy Wasdell ranked among the best of them. A war-time outfielder-first baseman with the team, Wasdell had a penchant for performing the unusual.

Once, before joining the Phillies, he set a major league record with four errors in one game. Another time, he charged a bunt, then hiked the ball through his legs to first like a football center (the second baseman wasn't covering the bag, and the ball rolled down the right field line, earning Wasdell a trip back to the minors).

Perhaps Wasdell's crowning achievement came while the Phillies were riding a train during a road trip. Vince DiMaggio, of the famed DiMaggios of San Francisco, was exercising his vocal cords with melodious notes that traveled through the car.

Wasdell didn't like DiMaggio's singing. Thought it disturbed his card game. Thought Vince should desist. With that, he got up and socked the unsuspecting warbler, sending him sprawling to the floor. For that show of power, the Phillies suspended Wasdell for three days.

An Easy Decision

Pitcher Schoolboy Rowe was about as crafty as they came. This was especially true when he hurled with the Phillies during the twilight of his career.

Schooly, who won in double figures four years in a row with the Phillies, had a knack for knowing when to get out of a game. If his arm got stiff, he had pitched five innings, and his team was winning, Rowe would exit the mound. If the arm got stiff and the Phils were losing, the big right-hander would stay in the game.

Rowe was also an excellent hitter. In 1949 when the Phillies bashed five home runs in one inning, Rowe (along with Andy Seminick who hit two, Del Ennis, and Willie Jones) was one of the bashers. Rowe had been particularly helpful to Ennis when the young slugger joined the Phillies in 1946.

On days when he wasn't pitching, Schoolboy—real name Lynwood—would sit on the bench and pick up pitches by observing opposing hurlers' motions. Then he would relay the pitch to Ennis by whistling—one whistle for a fastball, two for a curve.

Brotherly Love?

In 1947, in his first year in the major leagues, Jackie Robinson was the subject of widespread abuse from racist opponents and fans. None gave the major leagues' first African-American player in the 20th century more grief than the Phillies.

Led by Tennessee-born manager Ben Chapman, the Phillies had razzed Robinson well beyond the limits of civility in the club's first meeting of the season with the Brooklyn Dodgers at Ebbets Field. A black cat was released, and racist taunts from the Phillies' dugout were indicative of the extreme bigotry of the Philadelphia team.

Several weeks after their disgusting demonstration in Brooklyn, the Phillies were scheduled to play host to the Dodgers in an early May series at Shibe Park. But Phillies general manager Herb Pennock and his cohorts had other plans.

Right before the series was to start, Pennock telephoned Dodgers general manager Branch Rickey, the man who had pioneered Robinson's entry into the big leagues, and tried to assert his humanistic limitations.

"You just can't bring the nigger here with the rest of the team," Pennock warned. "We're not ready for that sort of thing in Philadelphia. If that boy is in uniform when Brooklyn takes the field, we will not play the game."

Rickey needed but a mere moment to respond. "Very well, Herb," he said. "If you don't field a team, we'll be happy to claim a 9-0 forfeit."

But Pennock didn't give in easily. He had someone in his office speak to the management at the Ben Franklin Hotel where the Dodgers stayed. When the team arrived, it was turned away. We won't admit "no ball club nigras," some hotel flunky said. After a lengthy search, the Dodgers finally found that the Warwick Hotel would take them.

So the Dodgers had a place to stay and a game to play. That Sunday, a doubleheader between the Phillies and Dodgers drew an all-time Shibe Park record of 41,660 fans. A large number of them were there to see for the first time one of baseball's most exciting players.

Right You Are, Ty

It was never any secret who resided in a place called Egypt, Pennsylvania. That was the home of a high school pitcher with extraordinary talent.

Curt Simmons seldom struck out fewer than 15 batters in a game. His high school team won three league championships, and his American Legion club captured two state titles. All the big league teams wanted him. But none craved his services more than the Phillies.

To get the inside track, team owner Bob Carpenter sent—can you imagine this?—a team of Phillies players to Egypt to face Simmons and his friends in an exhibition game. Curt struck out 12 Phils in a game that ended in a 4-4 tie. Ultimately, the 18-year-old phenom signed with the Phillies for a then club-record $65,000 bonus. Then, pitching for the Phils in the last game of the 1947 season, he beat the heavy-hitting New York Giants 3-1.

Simmons went on to a splendid 20-year big league career, winning 193 games. But it might not have happened if Curt had listened to Ty Cobb. While appearing in a high school All-American tournament at the Polo Grounds in his senior year in high school, Simmons pitched and played the outfield to help a team managed by Babe Ruth defeat a squad piloted by Cobb.

Cobb was so impressed with the youngster that he had this advice for him: "Better stick to the outfield where you can play every day."

Ready, Willing, and Able

Throughout his career, Robin Roberts was always a pitcher who was ready to pitch. Seldom missed a turn. Seldom asked for a day off. Give him the ball, and he just headed to the mound.

Between his first full season with the Phillies in 1949 through 1960, he started 40 or more games seven times. In those 12 years, he never started less than 35 games.

Like a Boy Scout, Robbie was always prepared to pitch. That trait was evident on his very first day in the major leagues.

In July 1948, Roberts was pitching with the Wilmington Blue Rocks in the Class B Interstate League. The team was playing in Hagerstown, Maryland, when the call came to send the young right-hander up to the big time.

Roberts hurried back to Wilmington, packed his belongings, and the next day took the train to Philadelphia, arriving at 4:30 p.m. By the time, he had reached the clubhouse at Shibe Park, it was 6 p.m. The Phillies were scheduled to meet the Pittsburgh Pirates at 8 p.m.

Soon after he'd arrived, Roberts was approached by Phils manager Ben Chapman.

"How do you feel?" the skipper asked.

Roberts told him he was fine.

"Good," Chapman said. "You're pitching tonight."

"I was nervous," Roberts recalled. "Never been so nervous in my life. But I thought Shibe Park was the prettiest ballpark I ever saw."

Although he allowed just five hits, Roberts lost his first start 2-0. But he was ready when needed. And that was a quality that Roberts carried with him throughout his Hall of Fame career.

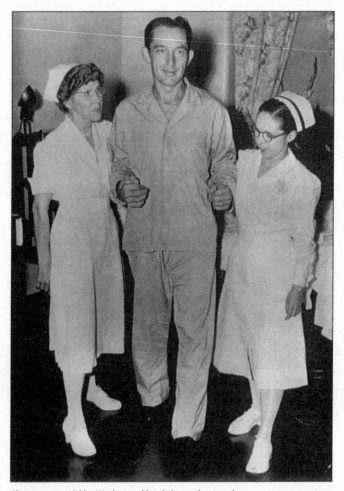

Shooting victim Eddie Waitkus couldn't believe what was happening. *Courtesy of Rich Westcott*

Not Funny

Despite Eddie Waitkus's outwardly serious demeanor, he was a man with a keen sense of humor. He was also quite a scholar, who it was said was fluent in five different languages.

In 1949, having just come to the Phillies that year from the Chicago Cubs, Waitkus was off to a strong start, toting a .306 batting average into mid-June. But on the night of June 15, Waitkus met with disaster in a Chicago hotel room.

Having had dinner with teammates Bill Nicholson and Russ Meyer, Waitkus was about to go on a date with a local college student when he received a note. It was from a girl who said that she was from Eddie's hometown of Cambridge, Massachusetts, and had some important news for him. She wondered if Waitkus could stop by her room at the hotel.

Waitkus, a bachelor, thought it was some kind of joke. But curiosity got the best of him, and he went to the room anyway. Once he was inside the room, the girl invited Waitkus to sit down. Then she walked to a closet and pulled out a .22 rifle. Waitkus still thought it was a joke.

"I was laughing when she shot me," Waitkus said later.

But it was no laughing matter. The girl—a crazed 19-year-old Chicago secretary named Ruth Ann Steinhagen—shot Waitkus in the chest, the bullet passing through a lung and lodging in his spine. It turned out that the girl had a secret crush on Waitkus.

Waitkus's life nearly ended. But he held on, and with the help of Phillies trainer Frank Wiechec, who put Waitkus through a vigorous rehab program that winter, the fancy-fielding first baseman returned in 1950 to help the Phillies win the National League pennant.

Waitkus died prematurely in 1972 at the age of 53. He was the model on whom the movie *The Natural* starring Robert Redford was patterned. Meanwhile, Steinhagen spent some time in an institution, but now lives in seclusion in Chicago.

Chapter 5

A Temporary Surge

1950-1959

Better Than Anybody

U nlike many of their predecessors, the Phillies of the 1950s at least had a measure of success. The club won the National League pennant in 1950 and had four other seasons in which it was .500 or above.

Unquestionably, winning the 1950 pennant was the highlight of the decade for the Phillies. It was the team's first flag in 35 years. It was won in dramatic fashion on the last day of the season after the Phils had held a seven-game lead in mid-September.

The 1950 Phillies were one of the most popular Philadelphia teams ever to grace a major league diamond. The club had two future Hall of Famers—pitcher Robin Roberts and center fielder Richie Ashburn—it had one of the league's best sluggers in Del Ennis, and it had a number of other key players. The Whiz Kids, as they had been named, met the vaunted New York Yankees in the World Series. No one was surprised when the tired and youthful Phils were swept in four games.

With their collection of fine young players, the Phillies were expected to be a National League front-runner for years to come. It didn't happen. With major slumps and egos standing in the way, the overconfident Wuz Kids tumbled all the way to fifth place in 1951. They could do no better than fourth the following year, despite only four fewer wins than the 1950 club.

The Phillies' time in the spotlight was over. As the decade wore on, the team got worse. Most of the former Fightin' Phils had been traded, only to be replaced by those of lesser skills. By 1958, the Phils were back in the basement, where they would stay for four straight seasons.

"For that one year, though, we were better than anybody," Roberts said. "I was disappointed that we were never able to win a pennant again."

So, too, were many others.

20 and Counting

If Robin Roberts had ever chosen to run for mayor of Philadelphia, he probably would have won by a landslide. To a generation of Phillies fans, the personable Roberts was that popular.

Robbie, of course, was no slouch when he had a ball in his hand, either. He won 286 games during a splendid career that reached its apex when he was elected to the Hall of Fame. He was a 20-game winner for the Phillies six times in a row, and he was the winning pitcher with a complete-game, 10-inning, five-hitter in the Whiz Kids' memorable 4-1 pennant-clinching victory in 1950. That, his third start in five days, was arguably the gutsiest pitching performance in Phillies history.

In the spring of 1952, Roberts, having won 41 games in the two previous years, had a terse meeting with owner Bob Carpenter. Naturally, money was the featured topic.

"I'm paying you to win 20 games," Carpenter intoned.

"Don't worry," Roberts retorted, "by the end of the year, I'll have them."

For Robin Roberts, it was 25 down and three to go. *Courtesy of Rich Westcott*

When the numbers were totaled at the end of the season, they showed Roberts with 28 wins. It was the most wins for a Phillies pitcher since 1917. It was also the highest total in the major leagues since Dizzy Dean won 28 in 1935.

The Undertaker as a Coach

Any time Jim Konstanty needed help with his pitching, he'd turn to his friendly undertaker. The undertaker knew exactly what made Konstanty's pitches work—or not work.

In 1950, the chunky, bespectacled hurler became the first relief pitcher to win a Most Valuable Player award. He won 16 games and saved 22 others while appearing in a then-record 74 games with the pennant-winning Phillies.

Konstanty was a starter through most of his early career, but not a particularly effective one. After joining the Phillies in 1948, Konstanty became a full-time inhabitant of the bullpen, except on one memorable occasion when he started the first game of the 1950 World Series.

Whenever Jim needed advice on his pitching, he turned to his friend Andy Skinner. Skinner was an undertaker in upstate New York who never played baseball and who knew very little about the game before he met Konstanty. But he figured out what made pitches do the things they did, and he became Jim's private pitching coach. Any time the reliever had a problem, he would call on Skinner, who would then pack his catcher's mitt and hurry to the aid of his old buddy.

Konstanty lacked a blazing fastball and all the other fancy pitches that comprise the repertoire of many pitchers. His specialty was a slider.

"He could hit you between the eyes with his best pitch and not give you a headache," snarled New York Giants manager Leo Durocher.

◆ ◆ ◆

To see him on the street, one might never guess that Konstanty was a big league pitcher. A schoolteacher maybe. Or even an accountant. But a baseball player? Hardly.

Jim had been a stellar four-sport athlete at Syracuse University, working his way through his four years there. Some years later,

Jim Konstanty throws while his private coach, Andy Skinner, watches. *Courtesy of Rich Westcott*

Konstanty was approached by a fellow alumnus, who asked if he remembered a particular classmate.

Konstanty said he didn't.

"Sure you must remember him," the Syracuse grad said. "He was an ATO."

"That lets me out," Jim responded. "I was an IOU."

Short Fuse

Few pitchers ever had a hotter temper or were involved in stranger incidents than Russ Meyer. That's why they called him "Mad Monk." Meyer, who pitched for the Phillies from 1949 to 1952, had more than his share of unusual episodes.

Players used to put snakes and dead birds in Meyer's locker because he was afraid of them. Once, he required 10 stitches in his nose after a girl with whom he was breaking up bit him. He punched a photographer for taking his picture. He fell to his knees and pounded the rubber after yielding a home run.

There was the time that Meyer, then hurling with the Brooklyn Dodgers against the Phillies, heaved a rosin bag some 60 feet in the air as he was walking off the mound after being taken out of a game. The bag landed squarely on his head.

While pitching with the Phillies, Meyer was lifted in an unusual manner by then-coach Maje McDonnell.

"It was the first time I ever took a pitcher out of the game," McDonnell recalled. "The manager usually did that. It was a sign of authority. But this time, Monk was getting knocked around, and Eddie Sawyer was so disgusted with him that he said, 'Maje, go get him. I don't want to look at him.'

"I said, 'You sure?'

"He said, 'Go get him out of there.'

"So I walked out to the mound, and said, 'Monk, you're out of the game. Gimme the ball.'

"He said, 'Here it is. Stick it up your ass.'

"I said, 'Well, the way you're going, it's a lot safer there.'"

Who Needs Sleep?

The Phillies of the 1950s had a roster that was filled with colorful characters. One was third baseman Willie Jones, aptly nicknamed "Puddinhead."

When Jones reported for his first spring training in 1947, he came to camp out of shape and well above his playing weight.

"He must have trained on corn pone and beans," fumed manager Ben Chapman.

Later, Jones was noted for bending the elbow. He bent it a little too much one night in Chicago and wound up getting arrested. It was 2 a.m. when Willie called Maje McDonnell and asked him to come to the police station to identify him.

"They don't know me here," Jones said.

"When I got there, Willie was sitting on the captain's desk, and they're all drinking beer," McDonnell said. "One of the cops had come in late, knew him, and identified him. I walked in, and he said, 'Maje, have a beer.' We had a doubleheader later that day. I finally got him out of there and brought him to the hotel."

Another time when the Phillies had a Sunday doubleheader in Philadelphia, Jones arrived at the ballpark lacking his game face. In those days, players didn't have to be at the ballpark on Sundays until noon because they were allowed to go to church first.

"Jones wasn't feeling too well," McDonnell remembered. "He looked terrible. We told him to lie down on the table and go to sleep. He slept for about an hour. When he woke up, we called the trainer, Frank Wiechec, in, and [Frank] gave him a rubdown. We threw Willie under the shower. Then he went out and took batting practice. He was a little woozy. We told him to go back in and sit by his locker. The game started about an hour later. Willie went five-for-nine in the doubleheader. A triple, two doubles, and two singles."

◆ ◆ ◆

Willie once told a writer that he was going to call his wife, who was traveling in Canada, and ask her to come home. Mrs. Jones was in her ninth month of pregnancy. Willie didn't want the child to be born in Canada.

"So what?" the writer asked. "Well, if he's born in Canada," Jones drawled, "he won't be able to grow up to be President of the United States."

Comic Relief

Without a doubt, the most memorable home run in Phillies history was struck by Dick Sisler in 1950. The 10th-inning blast gave the Phils the National League pennant with a 4-1 victory over the Brooklyn Dodgers on the last day of the season.

Sisler was the son of Hall of Famer George Sisler, who at the time of the homer was a scout with the Dodgers and seated in the stands at Ebbets Field. The manager of the losing Brooklynites was Burt Shotton, the skipper of the Phillies two decades earlier.

It wasn't common knowledge, but Sisler had a sizeable sense of humor. He also stuttered. Once, Dick drove his car into a gas station.

"Fi-fi-fi-fill 'er up," the Phillies' left fielder stammered.

"You—you—you w-w-want me to f-f-f-fill 'er up?" the attendant replied.

"A-a-a are yo-yo-yo-you making f-f-fun of me?" an irritated Sisler asked.

"Na-na-na-no," the guy said. "I st-st-st-stutter, too."

They both roared with laughter.

◆ ◆ ◆

Baseball players have always been noted for their willingness to pull pranks. Sisler, a master of comic relief, ranked among the league leaders.

In New York, the Phillies usually rode the subway to the ballpark. Sisler often carried on a loud conversation with one of the Phillies seated at the other end of the car.

"Hey, how are you doing?" somebody would yell to Dick. "How's the family?"

"Well, not so good," Sisler would reply. "My wife's been running around, and I'm taking care of the kids."

The other passengers would stop what they were doing and listen to the conversation, not knowing that these were two players fooling around. The conversation would continue. Eventually, the other riders would figure out the scheme.

Sometimes in spring training when the Phillies went to a restaurant for dinner, other players would tell the waitress that Sisler was hard of hearing. When she went to take Sisler's order, he'd yell, "What did you say? Ham and eggs? No, I don't want ham and eggs."

"Well, what do you want?" the waitress bellowed.

Soon, the two were screaming back and forth with all the other dinner patrons staring in amazement.

The Wrong Cadillac

There used to be a time when owning a Cadillac was a status symbol for ballplayers. A number of Phillies players drove them. Shortstop Granny Hamner was one of them. So was Willie Jones.

Phillies owner Bob Carpenter was always concerned about his players' welfare, so he tried to stay on top of their off-field activities. To this end, one season he hired a private investigator to keep tabs on Jones. Carpenter wanted the player followed for 10 days.

On the first day, the sleuth spotted a Cadillac leaving the ballpark and quickly pulled out, keeping an inconspicuous distance behind it. Only trouble was, it was the wrong Cadillac. This one belonged to Hamner.

With the unsuspecting detective following, Hamner drove toward his home in Northeast Philadelphia. Every turn he made, the snoop made it, too. Soon Hamner became suspicious. At one point, he made a stop, and the guy parked a few houses behind him.

Finally, Hamner arrived at his home, still being tailed. As he got out of his car, Granny noticed that the PI had parked across the street. By now, of course, the fiery Hamner had had it with the guy. He went into his house, got a gun, and walked around the side of the house and up to the car.

Hamner pointed the gun through an open window right at the investigator's head.

Broadcaster Gene Kelly has a word with Whiz Kids (from left) Willie Jones, Granny Hamner, Dick Sisler, and Del Ennis. *Courtesy of Rich Westcott*

"What are you doing?" Hamner demanded to know. "I'm going to kill you."

The man told Granny that he'd been hired to follow Willie Jones.

"Well, I'm not Willie Jones, I'm Granny Hamner," the shortstop said, "and I'm taking you to the police station."

The next day, the story made big news in the local papers. "Hamner Gets Man Following Him," one headline blared. Hamner also got the detective fired.

Out and Back

Andy Seminick was not only one of the top catchers in Phillies history, he was also one of the club's most popular players. A rugged guy with bulging muscles, Seminick was never too far from the spotlight when he played with the Phils.

Seminick hit two home runs in one inning in 1949 off former teammate Ken Raffensberger and the Cincinnati Reds. Three other Phils—Del Ennis, Willie Jones, and Schoolboy Rowe—also homered in that inning. The sturdy backstop hit another dinger later in the game.

Andy, who had escaped a life of work in the coal mines to become a professional baseball player, once played with a fractured ankle. He engaged in a memorable fight with Bill Rigney of the New York Giants. And he was the steadying hand behind a young pitching staff that helped the Phillies win the 1950 National League pennant.

The Phillies traded Seminick to the Reds in the winter of 1951 in a seven-player deal that among others brought catcher Smoky Burgess to Philadelphia. Seminick returned to the Phillies in 1955 in another swap with the Reds. Who did the Reds get in this six-player deal? None other than Smoky Burgess.

Foul Play

It would take a heap of digging to find a player more adept at fouling off pitches than Richie Ashburn. The Phillies' center fielder could slap foul balls with the best of them.

Ashburn was known to have fouled off 14 pitches in a single at-bat. His most famous foul balls were hit during a game in 1957.

As he often did until he got a pitch he liked, Ashburn smacked a foul liner into the third base stands. There, it struck a spectator square in the nose. Her name was Alice Roth, and she was the wife of Earl Roth, then the sports editor of the *Philadelphia Evening Bulletin.*

The unfortunate Mrs. Roth received emergency treatment for a broken nose and then was carried out of the stands on a stretcher. As she was being carried to an emergency room, Ashburn fouled another ball into the stands.

Who did it hit? Mrs. Roth, of course.

Balls hit by Richie Ashburn could sometimes be dangerous. *Courtesy of Rich Westcott*

◆ ◆ ◆

If it helped his hitting, Ashburn was never one to let an opportunity pass. The Hall of Fame outfielder was constantly in search of ways to give him the edge.

In one game during the mid-1950s, Sal Maglie was pitching for the New York Giants against the Phillies. Maglie, who was nicknamed "The Barber" because he was never reluctant to deliver a pitch under a batter's chin, was about as mean as any pitcher around. He could wither a batter just with his scowl.

Ashburn waited in the on-deck circle as Maglie warmed up at the start of an inning. As each pitch came in, the two-time batting champion took a swing with his bat.

When Ashburn went to bat, Maglie's first pitch came straight for his head. As he sprawled in the dirt, Ashburn heard The Barber grumble, "Nobody times my pitches."

Animal House

For various reasons, the Phillies always maintained a close connection with the animal kingdom. In the best of times, the team was said to have enough horses to win. In the worst of times, the club was described as a flock of turkeys.

Over the years, numerous players bore the nicknames of animals. Jim Owens was called "Bear." Frank Thomas was known as "Donkey." Roy Sievers went by "Squirrel." Don Hoak answered to "Tiger." Tom Glaviano was dubbed "Rabbit." Ken Silvestri owned up to the name of "Hawk." And Greg Luzinski was dubbed "Bull."

A 1950s infielder named Solly Hemus was called "Mighty Mouse." The Phillies of Hemus's era more closely resembled Minnie Mouse. At one point, though, the team had a nice long winning streak. Hemus had a ready explanation.

"Even monkeys fall out of trees once in a while," he advised.

At the end of the decade, another infielder named Joe Koppe joined the Phillies. Once during the 1959 season, umpire Ed

Runge was razzing Koppe, a hunting enthusiast whose real name was Joseph Kopchia, about his meager batting average.

"You're a terrible hitter," Runge untoned. "If somebody threw you an elephant, you couldn't hit it."

"Ed, if somebody threw me an elephant," Koppe shot back, "you couldn't call it."

Spoofing the Skipper

When he piloted the Phillies in the late 1950s, Mayo Smith contradicted standard managerial practice. He held meetings every day to go over the opposing team's hitters.

"Now on this guy," Smith would say, "you have to keep the ball down. Give him breaking stuff. On this guy, throw him the high hard one inside."

Pitcher Herm Wehmeier, a seasoned comedian, listened with amusement to the manager's spiel. One day, he said, "Everything [Smith] says, I'm going to say the opposite."

Smith got to the first batter, and said, "This guy loves breaking balls."

"You have to give him hard stuff," Wehmeier responded. "When I was with the Reds, we got him out with hard stuff."

"Well," Smith said, "we can try that."

When the game started, the first six batters the Phillies faced hit safely. By then, Smith knew he'd been had.

Costly Neglect

It took the Phillies a long time to learn the meaning of civil rights. The franchise was the last National League team to sign African-American players. It didn't happen until 1956, long after Jackie Robinson had made his major league debut.

Without black players, the Phillies fell far behind the teams that had a clearer vision of racial equality. Thus, when it came to the standings, the Phils were no match for teams such as the Brooklyn

Dodgers, New York Giants, and Milwaukee Braves, teams that had signed goodly numbers of black players.

The first black player to wear a Phillies uniform was the appropriately named John Kennedy, a light-hitting shortstop from the Kansas City Monarchs. He joined the team in spring training in 1957 and then appeared as a late-inning defensive replacement in five games at the start of the regular season. The first black regular with the Phillies was another shortstop, Chico Fernandez, a Cuban who came to the team in a trade with the Dodgers late in spring training in 1957.

It wasn't that the Phillies hadn't had a chance to sign black players before Kennedy and Fernandez came along. In the 1940s, native Philadelphian Roy Campanella had often tried to get the club interested in his services. He was always turned away. So was Hank Aaron, who came to Philadelphia for a tryout, but never again heard from the Phillies.

Clothesless in Pittsburgh

In the late 1950s, the Phillies had an assemblage of hurlers who were known almost as much for their nocturnal habits as they were for their mastery of the fine art of pitching.

They were called the Dalton Gang. When the gang rode into town, all residents were urged to take cover.

The gang's primary members were Dick Farrell, Jim Owens, Jack Meyer, and Seth Morehead—hell-raisers, one and all. Play at night, party later that night seemed to be their motto. Trouble was their trademark.

Each member of the quartet was followed by a trail of stories that told of his off-field exploits. One particular story involved Meyer, a hard-throwing reliever affectionately called "Gooneybird" by his pals.

The Phillies were on a short road trip that included just three games at Pittsburgh. For a short series like that, players back then seldom took a change of clothes. (You can make your own judgment on that.)

Heavy rain had caused cancellation of the Saturday afternoon game, and the players planned to have an early dinner before sampling the Steel City's nightlife. Meyer took a nap before the festivities began. Big mistake. While he slept, Farrell and the others crept into the room and threw Jack's clothes out of the window.

A little while later, Meyer awoke. Discovering the absence of his garments, Jack raced in his undershorts to the hotel lobby, screaming about his lost apparel. Hotel guests stared incredulously. Finally, Meyer was directed to the dining room where he proposed a fight with his teammates.

"Sit down and have a drink," Meyer's roommate Farrell suggested. A few drinks later, Meyer, by then much calmer, ventured outside the hotel, still in his shorts. He found his clothes lying on the ground. Coat, tie, shirt, pants—not a single item was missing.

Meyer was an especially effective reliever—he once struck out six batters in a row—but, like every other pitcher, he didn't always have his best stuff. One day, Meyer was getting hit particularly hard. He called time and motioned to the second baseman.

"Talk to me," he urged. "My mind just snapped."

Chapter 6

Disasters Reign

1960-1969

No Laughing Matter

I t would be an absolute fabrication to say that the decade of the 1960s ranks among the Phillies' finest. Nothing, in fact, could be further from the truth.

The real truth is that the decade was one of the Phillies' most horrific. How else would you describe a decade in which the Phils lost 23 games in a row in one season and blew a six-and-one-half-game lead with 12 games left to play in another? No other team in baseball history can lay claim to such ignominious catastrophes.

It was bad enough that the 1961 team went to the well 23 straight times and came back empty 23 straight times. But to blow the pennant in 1964 by losing 10 games in a row at the end of the season in the greatest collapse in sports history is a disaster that exceeds the boundaries of belief. And it left scars on the souls of Phillies fans that to this day are still there.

Sure, the decade wasn't a total loss. After all, it had Gene Mauch. Who could ever top his act? It had some marvelous players in Dick Allen, Johnny Callison, Jim Bunning, Tony Taylor, and Chris Short. And it had a warehouse full of colorful characters, most of whom performed better off the field than on it.

But there's no escaping the obvious. The 1960s were a miserable decade that included just two first-division finishes, two sevenths, and two eighths, and a whole truckload of other disappointments coming from a team that had been expected to be among the National League's elite.

It was definitely not a fun period in Phillies history. As one ex-player put it when asked if there were any traces of humor during that period, "There wasn't anything funny about that ***** decade."

Living Longer

One of the most popular and respected managers in the long line of Phillies skippers was Eddie Sawyer. The former New York Yankees farmhand piloted the Phillies in two different stints, going from 1948 to 1952—during which time he led the Whiz Kids to the National League pennant—and from 1958 to 1960.

When Sawyer was rehired at midseason in 1958, the Phillies were headed for a string of four straight last-place finishes. Under Sawyer, the club occupied the cellar in 1958 and 1959 and would remain there the next two seasons.

Sawyer might have struck out as a manager in his second time around, but he was no dummy. He was a Phi Beta Kappa graduate of Ithaca College, had a master's degree from Cornell, and in the offseason was a professor at Ithaca.

Sawyer was especially smart when it came to learning the futility of managing the Phillies. So after one game of the 1960 season, he quit the job.

When asked why he packed it in that abruptly, Sawyer had a simple response.

"I'm 49 and I want to live to be 50," he said.

Just for the record, Sawyer lived until he was 87.

Dick Gets De-Listed

Dick Farrell was a guy who was never afraid of playing a little chin music with opposing hitters. A hard-throwing right-handed reliever, Farrell could come up and in with the best of them. Sometimes, he'd even plunk one in your ribs if he felt especially belligerent.

Another pitcher with similarly cantankerous genes was Don Drysdale, who hurled his way to the Hall of Fame with the Los Angeles Dodgers. Like Farrell, Drysdale often threw high and tight, a practice that tended to keep hitters from getting too cocky when they faced him.

One day, Farrell was showing his wares to the Dodgers when Drysdale came to bat. Farrell promptly induced his opponent to fly sprawling into the dirt with a pitch that nicked the L.A. moundsman.

On his way to first base, Drysdale had a message for Farrell.

"You're on my list, you SOB!" he screamed. "You're in my book!"

Sometime later, Farrell was traded to the Dodgers. It was time to face the music. Shortly after his arrival, Farrell—or "Turk" as he was known—slinked sheepishly up to Drysdale in the L.A. clubhouse and introduced himself.

"Oh, you're Farrell," Drysdale said matter-of-factly. "Well, you're off my list now."

With that, he pulled a book out of his locker, grabbed a pen, and scratched Farrell's name off of a long list of misbehaving opponents.

What a Deal

John Quinn was an astute general manager who ran the Phillies' baseball operations from 1959 to 1972. Although he swung a few clunkers during his time in Philadelphia, most of Quinn's trades were above the bar rather than below it.

In Quinn's first trade, he brought stellar outfielder Johnny Callison to the Phillies. In his final swap, he put Steve Carlton in a Phils uniform.

Another fine deal by Quinn landed second baseman Tony Taylor. One of the players the Phils gave up in the 1960 exchange with the Chicago Cubs was pitcher Don Cardwell. The Cubs must have thought they really fleeced the Phillies. In his first game with the Cubs, Cardwell pitched a no-hitter.

Safety First

The Phillies hit rock bottom in 1961. In fact, no other team ever hit a rockier bottom.

En route to a 107-loss season under second-year pilot Gene Mauch, the 1961 Phillies lost 23 games in a row. No other big league team ever lost that many games in succession.

The Phils finally ended the wretched streak by winning the second game of a doubleheader at Milwaukee. That night, the club flew home to Philadelphia. As the airplane taxied up to the terminal, a large crowd of fans, ostensibly gathered to greet the return of the conquerless heroes, could be seen on the runway.

Peering out a window as the players were about to alight, pitcher Frank Sullivan had some special advice for his teammates.

"Leave the plane in single file," he implored, "so they can't get us all with one burst."

But Could She Pitch?

Not only was Gene Mauch a master strategist, he also had the habit of making scathing remarks. He had a keen sense of history, too. That might explain Mauch's assessment of two of his pitchers, Robin Roberts and Ferguson Jenkins.

In Roberts's final season with the Phillies, a year in which he went 1-10, Mauch justified his jettisoning the great hurler by claiming that "he throws like Betsy Ross." Several years later, after the Phillies incomprehensibly traded Ferguson Jenkins, Mauch, the history buff, defended the deal by asserting that "he throws like Dolly Madison."

Actually, there are no known records describing the pitching arms of either Ross or Madison. What is a matter of record, however, is that both Roberts and Jenkins are members of the Hall of Fame.

◆ ◆ ◆

Mauch was not a master of diplomacy. Called "The Little General" because of his Patton-like personality, he would do virtually anything to win. Such was the case one day when the Phillies' Bill White lofted a high pop foul above his team's dugout.

New York Mets catcher Jerry Grote clattered into the Phils' dugout, where he camped under the ball. As he was about to make the catch, Mauch whacked him across the arms. Grote, of course, dropped the ball.

At the time, Mauch's action was legal. But after the season, a new rule was written that required members of the opposing team to stand aside if a defensive player needed the space to make a play.

◆ ◆ ◆

Mauch's quick temper often got the best of him. Such was the case in 1963 when a Houston Colt 45s rookie named Joe Morgan beat the Phillies with a two-out, ninth-inning single.

"He looks like a Little Leaguer," Mauch fumed about the five-foot, seven-inch future Hall of Famer.

But that was just a warmup. When Mauch reached the clubhouse, where the usual postgame meal was spread out on tables, he wasted little time overturning the tables. Food, mostly spare ribs, barbecue sauce, and beverages, splattered everywhere, making a terrible mess. Some of it even landed on the clothes of outfielders Wes Covington and Tony Gonzalez. It was not Gene's finest hour.

"That was the day," he said later, "that the spare ribs went haywire."

Fiery Gene Mauch (right) seldom failed to make his point. *Courtesy of Rich Westcott*

On another day in Houston, this one when it was especially hot, Phillies players returning to the dugout after each half-inning on the field repeatedly complained about the bugs and the heat. Finally, Mauch got tired of hearing all of the bitching.

"I'm sick of you griping about the insects," he screamed. "They have to play in it, too."

A Real Fashion Plate

Ballplayers are often known for their sartorial splendor. Then there was Chris Short. He was a guy who, when he first reported to the Phillies as a raw rookie, lugged a cardboard suitcase that was packed with clothes from another planet.

The fine southpaw hurler, winner of 135 games during nearly 14 seasons with the Phillies, wore the nickname of "Styles." His favorite garment was a powder blue leisure suit, which didn't fit, but which he all-too-frequently draped around his frame.

"It's a nice-looking suit, don't you think?" Short once asked.

It was said that Short often went for days wearing the same clothes. Phils reliever Dick Farrell, a first-class funster, often got his kicks by cutting out the toes of Short's socks.

Have Another Drink

There was a time when a high-ranking member of the Phillies' front office (who, to protect the innocent, will not be mentioned by name) had an excessive familiarity with the substance that comes from a bottle. In fact, so familiar was he with that substance that it was often said that he held the club record for doubles.

In those days, the Phillies played at Connie Mack Stadium, where, among its many flaws, the park had a tiny, ultra-slow elevator that led to the press box high above the grandstand. The elevator was enclosed on three sides with a gate on the front. A cinderblock wall surrounded the elevator on all four sides.

Just before game time one day, two sportswriters, accompanied by the diligent drinker, rode the elevator up its small shaft. Our man, of course, had already paid a few visits to the sauce and he smelled quite unlike perfume. As the trio approached the press box level, the guy lurched into the control panel, accidentally hitting the stop button. Naturally, the elevator came to a premature halt. That didn't faze him one bit. He opened the gate—and walked straight into the wall.

Shaking himself off and rubbing his skinned nose, he turned to his two travel companions.

"This goddamn elevator never did work," he muttered.

◆ ◆ ◆

At about the same time, there was another upper-level Phillies executive who was also fond of beverages with strong flavors. This guy could nip with the best of them. His favorite players, people joked, were Jack Daniels and Jim Beam.

Following a rained-out game one day, he apparently stopped on the way home at virtually every watering hole he passed. After finally arriving home, he took a phone call from *Evening Bulletin* sportswriter Frank Bilovsky, who'd been trying to reach him for four hours. The two talked for several minutes, the guy making no sense as he babbled on and on. Eventually, the writer decided he had gotten nothing for his story and bid the guy goodbye.

"I appreciate your time," Bilovsky said.

"Yeah," the exec replied, "it was good seeing you."

The 200-Mph Fastball

The Phillies' record for most strikeouts in a nine-inning game is 17. The mark is held by right-hander Art Mahaffey, whose crackling fastball went largely untouched by Chicago Cubs bats during a game in 1961.

Reality suggests otherwise, but Mahaffey could often imagine himself as being the fastest pitcher of all time.

"When I was pitching, you warmed up at Connie Mack Stadium alongside the dugout on a mound right in front of the stands," he recalled. "The mound was so close to the stands that the ball would make a very loud noise when it popped into the catcher's glove. The noise was so loud that it sounded like the ball must have been going 200 miles an hour."

Mahaffey, a 19-game winner in 1962, also had a superb pickoff move to first base. When he first joined the Phillies in 1960, he predicted that he would pick off the first batter who reached base against him. Sure enough, he was right. While hurling against the St. Louis Cardinals in his first game, Mahaffey was touched for a hit by Bill White. Mahaffey promptly picked him off. He picked off the next batter to reach base against him, too.

Sleep-Watching

The parents of pitcher Cal McLish probably didn't do him a big favor when they named him Calvin Coolidge Julius Caesar Tuskahoma McLish. Writing that every time he had to sign an official document was enough to wear the poor guy out.

No doubt that explains why McLish was so drowsy the night he accompanied Richie Ashburn to a theater to see the Charles Lindbergh movie, *The Spirit of St. Louis.*

Because he was apparently slumber-deprived, McLish fell sound asleep as the flick began. He slept through the entire movie, not awaking until the very end.

"Let's get out of here," McLish urged as he emerged from his snooze. "This movie is boring."

Horse Sense

Among the great hitters who have worn the uniform of the Phillies, Dick Allen was surely one of them. Allen was a strong, sleek slugger who hit for distance and for high average. Many of his pokes, like the one that traveled 529 feet, were of particularly memorable quality.

Allen was originally called Richie. Then he went by Rich. Finally, he became Dick, a moniker that he carries to this day. By any name, though, Allen registered a set of impressive numbers. He clubbed 177 home runs in his six seasons with the Phillies, and his batting average rose above .300 four times. Eventually, he finished a 15-year career with 351 home runs and a .292 batting average.

Allen was also fiercely independent, a trait that sometimes got him in trouble.

Hits and horses were two of Dick Allen's best friends.
Photo courtesy of the Philadelphia Phillies

"I was a kind of Jesse James without guns," he once said.

Bizarre incidents plagued Allen during his days with the Phillies. He was involved in a controversial fight with teammate Frank Thomas. He severely injured his hand when he jammed it through a headlight while pushing his car. And while playing first base in his final months with the Phillies, he doodled in the dirt around the bag. "Boo," "Mom," and "Oct. 2" (the day he would be free to leave the Phillies) were some of the things he wrote.

Allen was such a lover of freedom—a trait that did not exactly charm the establishment in those days, but one that would be considered mild by today's standards—that he often drew criticism for his actions. The old-school attitude was expressed by George Myatt, a Phillies coach and interim manager.

"I don't think that God Almighty Hisself could handle that man," Myatt said.

Once, Allen, a lover and owner of horses, who could often be seen riding one of his steeds in Fairmount Park, was asked what he thought about playing on artificial turf.

"If a horse can't eat it," he said, "I don't want to play on it."

Ignoring Superstition

The first perfect game ever pitched in the National League and one of only 16 achieved since the pitching mound was located 60 feet, six inches from home plate, was hurled by a future United States senator. No other senator ever pitched a no-hitter, not even a Washington Senator.

In 1964, Jim Bunning, a three-time 19-game winner with the Phillies and owner of a previous no-hitter while with the Detroit Tigers, whitewashed the New York Mets in a game played at Shea Stadium. Appropriately, the event occurred on Father's Day. At the time, Bunning was the father of seven children (with two more to come later).

A future Hall of Famer, Bunning didn't believe in the age-old superstition of not mentioning a no-hitter when it is in progress. He kept track of the proceedings and constantly beseeched his teammates to help him out.

"Nine outs to go," he shouted. "Six to go." Then "Three to go." Along the way, he urged his teammates to make the plays. "Dive for the ball," he pleaded. "Don't let anything fall in."

After he completed the history-making feat, Bunning was invited to appear on *The Ed Sullivan Show*. He did, in the process knocking that day's U.S. Open winner, Ken Venturi, out of the show's spotlight. Later, Bunning and his family looked for a place to have dinner. Unable to find a suitable restaurant, the Bunnings wound up eating dinner on the New Jersey Turnpike at a Howard Johnson's. Such is the price of fame.

Jim Bunning (with general manager John Quinn) broke tradition while pitching a perfect game.
Courtesy of Rich Westcott

It Pays to Borrow

When it comes to outfielders, Johnny Callison was one of the Phillies' best. A fine all-around hitter, he was also a superb fielder with a terrific arm. And he had plenty of speed on the base paths.

One of the biggest moments in the lithe slugger's career came when he bopped a three-run homer in the bottom of the ninth inning to give the National League a 7-4 victory in the All-Star Game. The NL had begun the inning trailing 4-2.

Callison used a bat borrowed from the Chicago Cubs' Billy Williams to plant his dinger off Dick Radatz in the seats.

"It was lighter than mine," he said. "I got the ball, but Williams made me give the bat back."

Traded for Himself

Of the many shortcomings of the 1964 Phillies, one was certainly the club's lack of a first baseman. The club used nine different players at that position during the season. And that is not counting ballboys.

The Phils' drastic need for a first baseman was seemingly solved when the club picked up Frank Thomas from the New York Mets. But Thomas, after going on a hitting binge, broke his thumb in early September and was rendered useless for the rest of the season.

Back to the trading post the Phillies went. General manager John Quinn came up with a gem. He sent pitcher Marcelino Lopez and a player to be named later to the Los Angeles Angels for first sacker Vic Power. At the end of the season, Quinn announced the player to be named later. His name was Vic Power.

Gagging a Bat

In the mid- to late 1960s, the Phillies, desperate to win a pennant, stocked the team with veteran players. Most of them were obtained in trades. Most of them were also over the hill.

In their primes, people such as Dick Groat, Bill White, Harvey Kuenn, Dick Stuart, Lew Burdette, and Bob Buhl would surely have helped the Phils. But by the time they showed up in Philadelphia, the only thing they could help was their pension funds.

At the same time, the Phils also gathered a collection of oddballs, misfits, and loonies.

Other than serving as conversation pieces, their main contributions to the club appeared to come mostly in the form of comic relief.

There was Phil Linz, the harmonica-playing ex-Yankee. There was Bo Belinsky, the Hollywood smoothy who dated an assortment of prominent actresses. The list also included Jackie Brandt, Bob Uecker, and Lowell Palmer, who wore sunglasses when he pitched.

Then there was Bob Boozer. A relief pitcher with limited success, Boozer was quite the prankster. His favorite stunt was eating bugs and worms. He would often indulge his palate with such tasty critters while talking with other players and writers. The trick was—to use an old Midwestern expression—enough to gag a bat.

Same Old, Same Old

In the mid- to late 1960s, the Phillies might have been deprived on the playing field, but they hardly lacked colorful characters. One of them was outfielder Jackie Brandt.

A teammate once took the flaky Brandt to a store to get an ice cream cone. It was one of those stores that skirted the humdrum by offering 30 different flavors.

So what did Brandt order? One vanilla cone, please.

Master of the One-Liners

Although he spent less than two seasons with the Phillies, Bob Uecker left a trail of humor in Philadelphia. The backup catcher—usually deep backup at that—was a master of the one-liner. Here are some of those lines:

On joining the Phillies: "The cops picked me up on the street at 3 a.m. and fined me $500 for being drunk and $100 for being with the Phillies."

Comedian-catcher Bob Uecker was an authority on the Philadelphia boobird. *Photo courtesy of the Philadelphia Phillies*

On Philadelphia sports fans: "The fans are so rough that they boo kids who come up empty in the Easter egg hunt. They'd boo unwed mothers on Mother's Day. I've even seen people standing on street corners booing each other. One of my biggest thrills was watching a guy fall out of the upper deck at Connie Mack Stadium. The crowd booed when he tried to get up."

On the Phillies' practice site at their Clearwater spring training base: "It's like playing on Iwo Jima."

Uecker once fell into the dugout chasing a pop foul that was nowhere near where he thought it was. Another time, he chased a wild knuckleball pitch back to the screen, only to find out that the ball was lodged in the webbing of his glove.

Tough Glove

By the time he arrived for his one season in Philadelphia in 1965, Dick Stuart had acquired several nicknames. Two were "Dr. Strangeglove" and "Stonehands." Both were references to Stuart's distaste for balls that came his way at first base.

Stuart's reputation as a mishandler of thrown or batted balls was legendary. He could boot a ball with the proficiency of a cat trying to climb a tree. The man could hit—especially for distance—but playing defense? Not on your life, Bootsie.

"Errors," Stuart claimed, "are part of my image."

It was once said that Stuart was a "Williams kind of player. He bats like Ted and fields like Esther."

Dr. Strangeglove's aversion for balls reached an all-time low during a game in which Jim Bunning was the pitcher. After several pickoff attempts at first, Stuart wandered over to the mound.

"Don't throw it so hard," he begged Bunning.

Dick Stuart shows that he can actually hold onto a ball.
Courtesy of Rich Westcott

Chapter 7

On the Way Up

1970-1979

Yes, They Did

Years and years of frustration finally ended for the Phillies during the decade of the 1970s. It was a decade that launched the team into its finest era.

The Phillies moved into a new ballpark. A few years later, after enduring more misery during the early part of the decade, the team began to join the ranks of respectability. With young homegrown talent such as Mike Schmidt, Greg Luzinski, Larry Bowa, and Bob Boone, others such as Steve Carlton, Tug McGraw, and Garry Maddox who came in trades, and a hustling leader named Pete Rose, who came to the team at the end of the decade as a free agent, the Phillies became a club that was capable of reaching the top rung of the standings.

"Yes we can," a slogan initiated by mid-decade second baseman Dave Cash, became the team's rallying cry. And, yes, they did. The 1970s Phillies won three consecutive East Division crowns. They lost each time in the National League Championship Series—once to the Cincinnati Reds and twice to the Los Angeles Dodgers. But at least the team had finally shed the stigma of being a loser, a portrayal that had prevailed since 1950 and that had been magnified after the wreckage of 1964.

The Phillies had a genius named Paul Owens in the general manager's seat. They had an enterprising new president in Ruly Carpenter. They had a captivating new play-by-play broadcaster in Harry Kalas. And they had ballgirls, mascots, fireworks, dazzling side acts, huge crowds, and—best of all—an exciting team.

Wrecking Crew

After playing at Connie Mack Stadium (originally called Shibe Park) since 1938, the Phillies finally moved out of the 62-year-old ballpark following the 1970 season. The team would set up shop the next season in a venue in South Philadelphia called Veterans Stadium.

A big gala farewell was planned for the final game at CMS. The head planner was Bill Giles, then a Phils vice president and promotions specialist extraordinaire. Among many items on the agenda, Giles had decided to give to the first 5,000 fans entering the park wooden slats from stored-away seats that were used for repairs.

Giles's good intentions, however, backfired. From about the fourth inning on, a steady sound of hammering was heard in the stands.

"People were using [the slats] as hammers to remove everything they could from the stadium," Giles said.

The fans also had other instruments of mayhem. Some brought screwdrivers, wrenches, and even full toolboxes, all for the purpose of acquiring souvenirs from the expiring old ballpark.

"During the game, they [the fans] were taking chairs apart, taking the concession stands apart," Giles said. "They were even walking out with stuff from the restrooms. I saw one guy going down the street with a urinal."

Catcher on the Fly

As festive occasions go, Veterans Stadium's introduction to mankind was one of the finest ever staged in the city by the Delaware River. Virtually every imaginable kind of celebratory deed helped the new ballpark make its debut in 1971.

Politicians, celebrities, balloons, U.S. Air Force jet planes, speeches, the largest crowd at the time in Pennsylvania sports history, and even the general manager of the rival Montreal Expos arriving on a dogsled contributed to the gala celebration.

One of the best parts of the sideshow came when a helicopter flying over the stadium dropped the game ball to Phillies catcher Mike Ryan. Launched from several hundred feet up, the ball wobbled like a knuckleball through strong wind currents. Ryan struggled to get in position, weaving back and forth, trying to camp under the plummeting pill. The Phils' backstop finally made what was undoubtedly the toughest catch of his life.

A Wise Trade

Since the Phillies were rescued from the ashes of the late unlamented Worcester Brown Stockings, their pitchers have been on the high side of only nine no-hitters. Four of them occurred between 1885 and 1906.

One that was pitched after that period was the masterpiece turned in by Rick Wise in 1971. Wise not only no-hit the Cincinnati Reds, he also socked two home runs, the only time that's ever been done by a pitcher while he was throwing a no-hitter.

As the leader of the Phils' staff, Wise won 17 games that year for a last-place team.

At a banquet after the season, general manager John Quinn told Wise's wife, Susan, "We're never going to trade Rick Wise."

That winter, Wise was traded to the St. Louis Cardinals. It was a highly controversial swap that Phillies fans roundly criticized.

Told he wouldn't be traded, Rick Wise was traded. *Courtesy of Rich Westcott*

They wanted to know how could the Phils possibly deal the popular Wise for some guy named Steve Carlton.

The chief reason for the trade was that Wise was asking the Phillies for a substantial salary increase. Same for Carlton with the Cardinals. Because neither team wanted to give in, the trade was arranged. Ironically, both pitchers wound up getting from their new teams the raises they had sought from their old teams. And Carlton went on to become one of the top hurlers in Phillies history.

What No-Hitter?

The Phillies have always had their share of zany players. Guys who strayed a bit from the norm. Fun-loving guys. Guys who were maybe a couple of clowns shy of a circus.

Outfielder Roger Freed made a run at that status. Freed was a guy who was noted for eating chicken wings in a sauna. The year that Freed was acquired from the Baltimore Orioles, he was expected to hit 20 home runs. He hit six.

When Rick Wise pitched his no-hitter in 1971, Freed was playing right field. Wise also hit two home runs in the game as the Phillies won, 4-0.

After John Vukovich made a spectacular catch at third base on Pete Rose's line drive for the final out of the game, Phillies players danced gleefully off the field. Freed sidled up to Wise.

"Great hitting, Rick, great hitting," he shouted.

A Prince Among Frogs

Steve Carlton was the greatest left-handed hurler ever to ascend to a Philadelphia pitching mound. He captured the Cy Young Award four times, and in a glittering career that spanned 24 years, 15 of which were spent with the Phillies, he won 329 games, making him just one of 22 pitchers ever to reach the 300-win mark.

Steve Carlton and general manager Paul Owens (right) were two of the Phillies' main characters in the 1970s. *Courtesy of Rich Westcott*

He was a 20-game winner five times with the Phillies and overall won in double figures 18 years in a row. Although he helped the Phillies win five division titles, two National League pennants, and one World Series, his finest season came in 1972 while toeing the rubber for one of the Phillies' worst teams.

The Phillies have had all too many bad teams, but the 1972 gathering of woebegones was particularly frightful. It won just 59 games, lost 97, and finished a humiliating 37 games out of first.

That season Carlton won 27 games. That's nearly 46 percent of his team's victory total. Find another pitcher who can match that feat, and you'll win an all-expenses-paid trip to Manayunk.

Owning Up

Of all the superb pitching Jim Bunning did while wearing the Phillies' colors, there was one pitch that didn't quite make the list of the hard-throwing right-hander's outstanding feats. It was the pitch he threw in 1971 that the Pittsburgh Pirates' Willie Stargell hit into the upper deck in right field at Veterans Stadium.

The titanic swat landed in the 600 level, then bounced down a runway. It was considered the longest ball ever hit at the Vet and was only one of two ever to land in the 600 level. To mark the blast, the Phillies placed a star on the seat where the ball landed.

A few years later, while Bunning was a minor league manager, he brought a group of his players to the Vet. Pointing out different landmarks around the stadium, Bunning motioned to the star in the right field bleachers, noting that a Stargell home run ball once landed there.

The players were suitably impressed.

"Who could've given up a home run that was hit that far?" one of the unsuspecting players asked.

"I did," replied Bunning somewhat sheepishly.

Icing the Cluck

Fistfights happen. They're not just a part of the hockey handbook, either. They even occur in baseball.

There was the time, for instance, when Phillies relief pitcher Dick Selma was complaining long and loud about a flight the team had just made. Grousing about the food, the service, the delayed flight, Selma took out his displeasure on Phils traveling secretary Eddie Ferenz, an amiable fellow who was a longtime fixture with the team.

Only Ferenz wasn't so amiable this time. After suffering Selma's tirade for too long, Ferenz had had enough. He belted Selma with a solid shot to the jaw. The pitcher landed in the conveyor belt for luggage.

Oh, by the way, Ferenz was an ex-minor league ice hockey player.

Or Is It Decibells?

The best general manager the Phillies ever had was Paul Owens, whose eye for talent and genius for making trades propelled the Phillies to their finest era. Owens took a pathetic team and turned it into one that reached the highest levels of the National League.

Along with building the Phillies' farm system into one of the best in the big leagues, Owens made trades that brought in players such as Garry Maddox, Tug McGraw, Dave Cash, Bake McBride, Manny Trillo, Jim Lonborg, Dick Ruthven, and John Denny. Those players and many other Owens acquisitions helped the Phillies to two World Series appearances and five National League Championship Series.

As good as he was in the area of player personnel, Owens was also an accomplished mangler of the English language. There was the time, for instance, when being taken home from the airport, Owens asked the driver to turn the car radio "up a few disciples." Later, when asked about his word selection, Owens replied, "I was just kidding. I knew it wasn't disciples. I knew it was decimals."

Another time, Owens was discussing his pitching staff. So-and-so is strictly a starter, he explained. So-and-so is strictly a reliever. The name Woodie Fryman came up.

"Woodie can go either way," Owens said. "He's that kind of fellow."

Reality Check

Sometimes, though not always, road trips can be tedious affairs. And the longer he's away, the less a player is caught up in the reality of home life.

The Phils were returning from a three-week sojourn, and as the airplane approached the landing strip, one of the players hollered, "Now don't forget your wives' names, men."

Quadruple Scotch

The great high-wire artist, Karl Wallenda, exhibited his breathtaking act twice at Veterans Stadium. In 1972 and again in 1976, he walked on a tightrope across the top of the stadium. That's one side to the other, rooftop to rooftop, high above the playing field.

For some, the act was too terrifying to watch. They had to leave their seats and hide. Actually, the stunt was no walk in the park for Wallenda, either, even though he stopped to do a handstand midway across the wire.

After returning from his trip to outer space, Wallenda sat down with the media. But before he took questions, he had one request. He asked for two glasses, with a double scotch in each.

Not a Scrapgoat

Nobody ever said that managers have to be specialists in the art of public speaking. They don't even have to be grammatical wizards. If they can put two or three coherent sentences together, that's usually enough.

One of the Phillies' all-time greats in the field of oral delivery was without question Frank Lucchesi, an extremely pleasant little fellow who wore his emotions on his sleeve. Lucchesi, whose term with the team went from 1970 to 1972, wept when he was hired. And he wept when he was fired.

Lucchesi was the Phillies' manager when the team played the Montreal Expos in the last game at Connie Mack Stadium. With bedlam reigning in the stands and the score tied at 1-1 after the ninth inning, Lucchesi and Expos pilot Gene Mauch agreed that the game would end after the 10th inning, no matter what.

But Oscar Gamble's single in the bottom of the 10th scored Tim McCarver from second to give the Phillies a 2-1 victory. As Gamble reached first, Lucchesi raced onto the field to celebrate. With fans virtually covering the field—some trying to tear out home plate, others pulling up pieces of grass—the manager rushed to Gamble to deliver a hug. The Phils outfielder brushed him off.

"Run, man, run like hell," Gamble screamed. "We'll be happy later."

Once, when asked about managing the lowly Phillies, Lucchesi replied, "You can't serve water with a pitchfork." During a lengthy slump, he said the Phillies "were in the doodlums." In a session with the media, the skipper, indicating that he preferred to stick to the subject at hand, advised that he "didn't want to go off on a transom." Another time, while bearing the brunt of a Phillies' losing streak, the man who called himself "Skipper," provided a special rebuttal.

"Nobody's going to make a scrapgoat out of me," he said.

Mr. Malaprop

Perhaps the master of the malaprop was Danny Ozark, Lucchesi's successor as Phillies manager. Ozark, who once swung at and missed a writer and who piloted the Phils to three division titles, could mangle a message with the best of them.

One time, during a conversation with a writer, Ozark blurted out, "You know I'm a fascist."

"You're a what?" said the writer.

"Not the Italian kind," Ozark replied. "The other kind. Somebody who says one thing and means something else."

Ozark was a little less facetious when he said that outfielder Mike Anderson's "limitations were limitless." He said that being swept in a series one weekend "was beyond his apprehension." Another time, while discussing a problem he was having at third base, he told listeners that "I don't want to get into a Galphonse and Astone situation at third base." When asked once about a morale problem on the team, he insisted that "on this team, morality is not a factor." Danny informed the press on one occasion that he had "a great repertoire with my players." And after a losing streak, Ozark explained the slump by saying, "Even Napolean had his Watergate."

Danny wasn't just a wordsmith. Once, he put one of those metal rings on a fungo bat, swung the bat, and the ring flew off and hit pitcher Randy Lerch square in the head. Another time, he was going to pull pitcher Wayne Twitchell, but slipped and fell on his way out of the dugout. Too embarrassed to continue, Ozark retreated to the dugout, where he watched Twitchell allow three more runs.

Ozark's math was occasionally flawed, too. After the Pittsburgh Pirates eliminated the Phillies with a victory that gave the Bucs a seven-game lead with six games left to play, Ozark disagreed with the obvious.

"We're not out of it yet," he advised. "If we win all our games, and they lose all theirs, we're still alive."

He was told, "You're seven down with six to play."

"Well, that's very disheartening," the resident mathematician replied.

If He Only Knew

Some pitchers enjoy a bit of conversation with their teammates when they're on the mound. While they're working, other pitchers wouldn't utter even one syllable to their own mothers.

Steve Carlton was a classic example of the latter. Not only would he not talk to anybody while he was pitching, he would not talk to almost anybody anytime.

This was something Ted Sizemore didn't know when he came to the Phillies in 1977. Apparently, the second baseman figured that Carlton was at least somewhat approachable during the heat of battle.

With that in mind, Mike Schmidt and Larry Bowa hatched a plan during an early-season game shortly after Sizemore's arrival. The plan called for initiating Sizemore into the ways of "Steve the Spinx."

"Lefty never liked anyone going to the mound to talk to him," shortstop Bowa said. "If you did, he'd tell you to worry about playing your position. And he wouldn't do it too politely, either.

Danny Ozark once claimed that "even Napolean had his Watergate."
Courtesy of Rich Westcott

"So in Size's first game with Lefty pitching, Schmitty and I decided to play a little joke. The first time Lefty walked someone, I kind of covered my mouth so Lefty couldn't see me and told Size to go to the mound. But Lefty turned around and saw Ted coming toward the mound, and told him in no uncertain terms not to take another step and go play second base."

Sizemore quickly retreated. As he did, he spewed a litany of profanities in the direction of Schmidt and Bowa, both of whom were practically laughing their socks off.

Worth the Price

Mike Schmidt was not only the best third baseman the Phillies ever had, he was the best third baseman Major League Baseball ever had. Schmidt could do it all—hit, hit with power, run, field, throw—the kind of guy the scouts call a "five-tool player."

Schmidt led the National League in home runs eight times, becoming one of just 17 major leaguers to hit 500 or more home runs in a career. He won 10 Gold Gloves. And he captured the Most Valuable Player award three times. Schmidt entered the Hall of Fame in 1995.

No less an authority than Pete Rose once said, "Mike was the greatest player I ever played with and certainly as good as any player I ever played against. Just to be able to rub elbows with Mike for five years in Philadelphia made my career worthwhile."

As good as he was, making the big leagues wasn't all that easy for Schmidt. When he was seven years old, he fell out of a tree, careening 24 feet to the ground while grabbing a 4,000-volt electric wire on the way down. It was a miracle that Schmidt wasn't electrocuted. Nor did he break any bones. Schmidt also had major knee surgery twice—once in high school and once in college. That made a number of scouts—excluding, of course, the Phillies' Tony Lucadello—shy away.

And get this. When he played at Ohio University, Schmidt was a shortstop. He was also a switch-hitter. He received a bonus of $35,000 when he signed with the Phillies in 1971.

A Grave Forecast

For most of his career in Philadelphia, Steve Carlton refused to talk to the media. Apparently, he was disturbed by a story a sportswriter penned and decided he had the right to remain silent.

Carlton wouldn't even talk to writers on an informal basis. Once, when asked by a writer if the two could just have an off-the-record chat, the southpaw refused.

"Policy is policy," he stated.

The role of mouthpiece for the silent wonder fell to Tim McCarver, Carlton's personal catcher. After every game, it was the job of the backup backstop to dissect the future Hall of Famer's performance and to answer the mostly uninspired questions hurled his way.

McCarver, who caught most of Carlton's games while the two were teammates, dutifully executed his role as the pitcher's spokesman.

"When Lefty and I die," he said, "they're going to bury us 60 feet, six inches apart."

◆ ◆ ◆

A practical joker of the highest level, McCarver was at spring training in Clearwater one year when he spotted a patsy. It was a young clubhouse boy who was new to the job.

"I need the key to the batter's box," McCarver said to the boy. "Go ask Kenny Bush [the clubhouse manager] for it."

The boy went to Bush, and then returned to McCarver empty-handed. Four times McCarver sent the unsuspecting kid back to Bush. And each time, he came back without the key.

◆ ◆ ◆

McCarver has another footnote attached to his name. During a game in 1970, his right hand was broken when it got in the way of a foul tip off the bat of Willie Mays. Mike Ryan entered the game as McCarver's replacement. A few minutes later while still in the same inning, Willie McCovey slid into the plate and into Ryan. The result? A broken hand for Iron Mike.

Two more catchers called up from the minors to replace McCarver and Ryan also suffered injuries. The Phils had to activate coach Doc Edwards, a former backstop.

When he signed with the Phillies, Mike Schmidt was a switch-hitting shortstop. *Courtesy of Rich Westcott*

A Mighty Single

Numerous home runs are considered among the longest Phillies players have hit. But what about the longest single?

It was hit by Mike Schmidt off Claude Osteen in 1975 at Houston. The blast struck a public address speaker hanging from

Tom McCarver never met a good prank that he didn't like.
Photo courtesy of the Philadelphia Phillies

the Astrodome roof. The speaker was 117 feet high and 300 feet from home plate.

When the ball bounced back onto the playing field, Schmidt had to settle for a loooong single. Nevertheless, the Phils won 12-0.

Not That Leo

Before he became a manager of some note, Davey Johnson was an excellent second baseman, performing with considerable skill, primarily with the Baltimore Orioles and Atlanta Braves. Johnson joined the Phillies in the twilight of his career, but he was still good enough to grab himself a spot in the club's record book. In 1978, he hit two pinch-hit grand-slam home runs, a feat that has never left the bat of any other Phils hitter.

Johnson was also a voracious reader. Or so he claimed. At least, he was enough of a reader that other players on the team often tore the last 10 pages out of his books. Johnson told teammates that he had even read *War and Peace*. When asked the name of the author, he had the answer right on the tip of his tongue.

"Leo Toystore," he said.

Pass the Mustard

Unquestionably, one of the Phillies' premier characters was a sweet-swinging outfielder who answered to the name of Jay Johnstone. J.J.'s hitting was about on a par with his comedy. He was very good at both.

Johnstone hit .329 one year and .318 another during his four-plus seasons with the Phillies. He and manager Danny Ozark never got along, and when Johnstone's name was missing from the starting lineup, fans would hang signs saying, "Play Jay Every Day."

Around the ballyard, Johnstone, who once visited a concession stand during a game to purchase a hot dog, was not so coincidentally known as a bit of a hot dog. In recognition of that characteristic, one season the Phillies presented him with a five-foot-long hot dog. There is no record of whether or not Jay ate the whole thing.

Premium Coverage

One of the best center fielders the Phillies ever had was a swift-footed, surehanded artist who roamed the outfield with the ease and grace of a greyhound. Any ball hit even remotely close to Garry Maddox was a sure F-8.

Maddox won eight Gold Gloves. Only Roberto Clemente and Willie Mays won more among National League outfielders. Maddox's career fielding record was a dazzling .983 over 15 seasons, nearly 12 of them spent with the Phillies.

Once, Maddox even got a putout at home plate. How? A base runner was trapped between third base and home. Back and forth he went, escaping the best intentions of Phillies fielders. Eventually, nearly the entire Phils defense had joined the fun. The runner was finally nailed at home with Maddox applying the tag.

Often called "The Secretary of Defense," Maddox was paid the ultimate compliment by then-New York Mets broadcaster Ralph Kiner. "Two-thirds of the earth is covered by water," Kiner said, "and the other third is covered by Garry Maddox."

Woman's Intuition

In the 1970s, the Phillies were one of the first teams to break the on-field gender barrier when they hired young women to serve as ballgirls. It was an attempt to add window-dressing to a game that shouldn't need it. Eventually it became politically incorrect to shower such attention on sweet young things who could neither hit, field, nor throw, and the practice—surely to the delight of NOW—was abandoned.

For the decade or so that it lasted, though, the Phils paraded a cabaret full of pulchritudinous ladies down the foul lines. One of the most attractive of them was a stunning blonde named Mary Sue Styles. Styles patrolled the left field foul line, and in due time, her good looks and strong throwing arm made her almost as well known as some of the Phillies players.

They called Garry Maddox "The Secretary of Defense."
Courtesy of Rich Westcott

Styles was very much into the game. For instance, in 1979 the Phillies and Pittsbuurgh Pirates were in a feverish battle for the division title. In a late-season game with two men on base, the Phils' Keith Moreland smashed a line drive down the left field line and into the stands. The night was misty, and despite poor visability, third base umpire Eric Gregg, after hesitating for a moment, signaled home run.

The call sent the visiting Pirates into orbit. Put another way, the Pittsburghers went crazy. At one point, Bucs coach Bill

Robinson—a former Phillie—pointed out that broadcaster Chris Wheeler had called the ball foul on television. Eventually, crew chief Frank Pulli, umpiring at second base that night, came over to Gregg.

"Hey big guy," he said, "that ball's foul. We have to turn it over."

Advised of the situation, home plate umpire Doug Harvey reversed Gregg's call.

That brought Phils manager Dallas Green storming out of the dugout, throwing a water bucket on his way and raising a ruckus like few ruckuses he'd ever raised. Green was soon asked to spend the rest of the game in the clubhouse.

After the game, which the Pirates won, Gregg defended his call. He said he saw Styles jumping up and down, waving her arms, so he figured it was a home run.

"If it was good enough for Mary Sue," Gregg explained, "it was good enough for me."

Some years later, Styles shared a little secret with Wheeler. She confessed that she wasn't wearing her contacts and didn't see the ball.

Good with the Shovel

Unlike their predecessors, modern players don't need offseason jobs. They can eke out a meager existence without them.

There are exceptions, though. The Phillies' first baseman in 1977 and 1978 was Richie Hebner. He gave the club two solid seasons of plus-.280 hitting. He also had an offseason job. Hebner dug graves back home near Boston. He was not only earning some spare change, he was also lending a hand—so to speak—to his father, the foreman of the cemetery.

Hebner, an All-America ice hockey player in high school who was offered a contract by the Boston Bruins, had one other unusual trait. It was said that he led the National League in getting free tickets for playoff games. And that was a lot of free tickets, considering Hebner played on division champions six different times.

Mr. Walkoff

It would be hard to locate a more fun-loving player than Tug McGraw. The Tugger enjoyed life to the fullest, and he seldom hesitated to demonstrate his gleeful demeanor.

"I could have fun in a stalled elevator," he said.

McGraw, of course, was a darn good relief pitcher, too. He saved 180 games during a 19-season career, including 94 in his 10 years with the Phillies. It is the fourth-highest total in club history.

There was a time, however, during a Sunday doubleheader at Pittsburgh in the late 1970s when McGraw was less than fine. In the first game, the Phils were winning, but in the bottom of the ninth, the Pirates had the bases loaded with two outs. The phone rang in the Phils bullpen, and a voice said, "Get McGraw ready." A moment later, manager Danny Ozark walked to the mound where he signaled for McGraw.

"Can't he stall?" asked McGraw, who had thrown only two pitches.

"He wants you. Go get 'em," bullpen coach Mike (Irish) Ryan replied.

McGraw sauntered to the mound where he took the customary eight tosses. Play then resumed. On Tug's first pitch, Pirates pinch-hitter Ed Ott slammed a grand slam to give the Bucs a walkoff victory.

Several hours later, the Phillies again took a lead into the bottom of the ninth. Again, the Pirates loaded the bases with two outs. Again, Ozark called for McGraw, who this time had thrown no pitches in the bullpen. Again, Ott stood at the plate waiting for McGraw to finish his warmup tosses.

"Don't worry, kid," Ozark assured, "lightning doesn't strike in the same place twice."

But it did. Ott drilled McGraw's first pitch over the wall for another grand slam. And the Pirates again had a walkoff win.

"When I got home," McGraw recalled, "my kids thought I had changed my name to Mr. Walkoff. When I went to the mall, they were calling me Mr. Walkoff and Mr. Slammer. My dad's prophesy came true. He had said, 'Son, the good news is, you're going to make it in the big leagues, and someday you're going to lead the league in grand slams.' The bad news is he forgot to tell me that I was going to be a pitcher."

See You Later

In their days as young upstarts, Dickie Noles and Kevin Saucier were good buddies. The two relief pitchers were also world-class hell-raisers. One time, that distinction almost got the best of them.

Noles and Saucier had been giving a pitching clinic at the Jersey shore and decided to stop and sample the offerings at Atlantic City. Time flew by, and thinking the Phillies had an afternoon game, the dynamic duo raced back to Philadelphia, fearful that they would arrive late.

When they finally reached the clubhouse, they were greeted by an unsettling sight. Nobody was there except utility infielder John Vukovich.

"Good grief," they thought, "everybody must be out on the field." After hearing their excuses, Vukovich made a pronouncement, "It's a night game, you dummies."

Chapter 8

Reaching the Top

1980-1989

Victory at Last

No decade in Phillies history ever began so gloriously as the 1980s. In the first year of the decade, the Phillies won the first World Series in the team's 97-year history. Then three years later, the Phils captured their fourth pennant.

The 1980 season was one that no Phillies fan who was conscious at the time will ever forget. Winning the East Division title followed a bone-jarring clubhouse tirade by general manager Paul Owens that snapped the team out of its late-season lethargy.

"You played the first five months for yourselves," Owens thundered. "You better stop your goddamn pouting. The last month is [team president] Ruly Carpenter's and mine."

The team clinched the National League pennant with a pulse-stopping victory in five games over the Houston Astros. Then the Phillies, under manager Dallas Green, advanced to the World Series, beating the Kansas City Royals, four games to two.

Steve Carlton earned two wins, Tug McGraw got one win and two saves, and Mike Schmidt snatched the Series MVP award after hitting .381 with two homers and seven RBI. The city went wild. Fans celebrated throughout the night, then two million of them showed up the next day to watch the Phillies' victory parade.

With Owens now managing, the Phillies won the National League pennant again in 1983 after downing the Los Angeles Dodgers in four games. LCS MVP Gary Matthews collected three home runs and eight RBI while batting .429. The Phils, however, fell to the Baltimore Orioles in five games in the World Series.

While it lasted, the Phillies had a spectacular run. But a decade that began so gloriously ended dismally as the team got above .500 only once more the rest of the decade and finished the 1980s as the division doormats.

Baseball's Slowest Fastball

No pitch in Phillies history is more famous than the one Tug McGraw threw to end the 1980 World Series. With it, McGraw struck out Willie Wilson of the Kansas City Royals for the final out of the sixth game.

McGraw's pitch came just one out after a foul ball hit in front of the Phillies' dugout by Frank White clanked off the glove of catcher Bob Boone and was caught just before it hit the ground by the ever-alert Pete Rose. Rose then showed how much of a pro he was. Instead of tipping his cap, strutting around, or patting himself on the back, he rushed to the center of the infield to make sure that all of the bases were covered so that no runners could tag up and advance after the catch.

Boone then went to the mound to visit McGraw.

"Isn't this exciting, Tuggles?" he said.

McGraw replied, "Boonie, you talk funny when you're nervous."

The bases were loaded when Wilson stepped to the plate. As policemen, some with dogs, others on horseback, lined the Veterans Stadium field in hopes of preventing over-jubilant fans

Tug McGraw might be about to deliver a Cutty Sark or a Bo Derek.
Courtesy of Rich Westcott

from tearing the place apart, McGraw went to a 1-2 count on the batter. He then fanned Wilson to end the game.

Asked after the 4-1 win what pitch he threw, McGraw, who admitted that he was totally out of gas and his arm was "killing" him, said it was "the slowest fastball thrown in the history of baseball."

Asked how he figured that, McGraw replied, "It took 97 years to get there."

◆ ◆ ◆

McGraw had entered the game in relief of Steve Carlton. When the Phillies starter began to falter in the seventh inning, the call went to the bullpen to get Tug ready. By then, the animal brigade had begun assembling.

"When I went to pick up my glove to start warming up," McGraw recalled, "a German Shepherd was resting and he had his head lying on my glove. I went to reach for it, and that was not the smartest thing in the world to do.

"So I told the cop, 'Hey, I gotta get my glove.'

"The cop reached down to get my glove, and there was slobber all over it. I don't know what they gave these dogs before the game, but it was stronger than what they gave the players. You can't spit with the stuff they give the players; it dries your mouth out. But this dog was drooling. It was all over my glove. The cop saw it.

"He said, 'Let me get a towel.'

"I said, 'Oh no, no it's fine. It might come in handy later.'

"I was just joking around. I never threw a spitter. But the cop thought it was real funny. It was a case of using a little bit of humor in a tense situation.

"So I was warming up, and then they took Lefty out, and I went in in the eighth with the bases loaded. I got out of the inning. We batted, and then we went out in the top of the ninth, and the dogs and horses were circling the field. Over behind the first base bag was a horse. After I got the first out, the horse lifted up his tail and took a big dump. I was thinking, 'If I don't get out of this inning, that's what I'm going to be.' I was thinking of the '64 Phillies, the negative fans, and all the other stuff. 'I have to pull this off. If I don't, I'm going to be Gene Mauch's neighbor next year.'

"I looked over at the dugout, and there was a dog right by Dallas Green. The dog was looking out at the mound and barking like hell at me. I saw it was the same cop who had tried to hand me the towel. So it was the dog that had had its head on my glove. And I was thinking to myself, 'That's the canine corps. This is the ninth inning and I need a K. This is like a signal from the baseball gods. All I have to do is deliver.' I struck Wilson out, and the first thing I did was look into the dugout, and that dog was jumping around and the cop was jumping up and down.

"I thanked the dog."

◆ ◆ ◆

Before one of the World Series games, McGraw was shagging flies in the outfield with his brother Hank, a former Phillies minor league player. The two were clowning around, catching balls behind their backs, something they did as kids back in California.

"All the sudden, a kid about 10 or 11 years old, wearing a little Phillies uniform, runs out of the dugout sprinting as fast as he can to center field," McGraw recalled. "He stood right next to us. A fly ball came off somebody's bat toward left-center field. Before Hank or I could even budge, this kid was off and running for it. He got to the warning track, stopped, turned around and faced the ball, and caught it behind his back, just like we were doing. The people in the stands went absolutely berserk. It was the biggest roar of the crowd I ever heard in a pre-World Series batting practice."

Who was this kid? Turns out his father was the Phillies catcher. Then, as now, the kid went by the name of Bret Boone.

◆ ◆ ◆

Nobody ever had more fun as a baseball player than McGraw. With Tug, fun was all part of the game. Lessen the tension. Enjoy yourself. Don't take everything so seriously. That's the way Tug looked at things.

McGraw applied his playful spirit to his pitches. He gave them all names. One was the Jamison fastball; it was hard and straight, like he liked his Irish whiskey. Another was the Cutty Sark, which, like the sailboat on the label, sailed. Then there was the Bo Derek—it had a nice little tail on it. The Peggy Lee was Tug's change-up. The hitter would swing, the ball wouldn't be there yet, and he would say, "Is that all there is?" When McGraw gave up a home run, he had thrown his Sinatra ball, "Fly Me to the Moon."

"When the writers came in after a game, they'd always want to know, what was that pitch, how did you hold it, what were you trying to do with it, blah, blah, blah," McGraw said. "I just started giving the pitches names, just to make it more fun to talk about. Make it more interesting, make it easier for all of us. The writers didn't like coming in every night and having to ask the same old questions and get the same old answers. So I tried to spice it up a little, make it more fun for everybody, including myself.

"I used to talk to myself on the mound. When I'm doing my pitch selection, I'd say, 'Give him the Jamison fastball. Let's give him the Cutty Sark; keep it inside.' It became part of my own thinking."

Difference of Opinion

Larry Bowa is probably the finest shortstop not in the Hall of Fame. A brilliant defensive player, the slick-fielding midfielder with the shotgun arm holds the National League record for the highest fielding percentage for a shortstop in a career (.980).

For a guy who, as a young professional, was not viewed as a particularly potent hitter, Bowa wound up his career with good marks with the bat, too. He had 2,191 hits and a lifetime batting average of .260. Not a bad career for a guy who was cut from his high school team three years in a row and who wasn't picked by anybody in the major league draft.

Bowa was never noted for his mild manner. He had a fiery demeanor, he was as feisty as a wounded crocodile, and he could sling a barbed comment that would make Don Rickles proud.

Whether on the field or off, Larry Bowa usually has an opinion.
Courtesy of Rich Westcott

During the 1980 season, Bowa unleashed his fury on Phillies fans. The notoriously negative Philadelphia fans had loudly booed the club after it lost a lead to the Chicago Cubs in a crucial late-season game. It didn't matter that the Phillies had come from behind to win in 15 innings. Bowa was furious.

"Those ***** front runners are the worst fans in baseball," he screamed after the game.

About one month later, the Phillies won the World Series, and the next day, they took part in a parade witnessed by two million people. When the parade reached JFK Stadium, its final destination, various players spoke.

"This is the greatest moment of my life," Bowa said, "and I'm glad I can share it with the greatest fans in baseball."

How Did He Taste?

The Phillies captured the National League pennant after a league championship series with the Houston Astros that has been generally considered the greatest LCS of all. The Phils won the series, three games to two.

In the fifth and final game of the series, the Phillies trailed 5-2, entering the eighth inning with Nolan Ryan on the mound for Houston. A five-run Phils explosion in the eighth put the Phils on top. Houston came back to tie before the Phillies won 8-7 on Garry Maddox's 10th-inning RBI double.

The big blow in the eighth for the Phillies was a two-run triple by eventual LCS MVP Manny Trillo that pushed the team to a 7-5 lead. Lee Elia, then the Phillies' third base coach, said later, "I grabbed Manny and said, 'I love you. I love you.' I didn't want to kiss him, so I bit him on the arm. Gave him a pretty good bite, too. Manny looked kind of startled."

Breaking the Ice

It has often been claimed (probably incorrectly) that a single pitch turned the whole 1980 World Series around. That was the fastball thrown by Dickie Noles that sent George Brett of the Kansas City Royals sprawling into the dirt in the fourth game of the Series.

Noles's knockdown missile flirted with Brett's skull, causing the future Hall of Famer to seek safety on his derriere. Afterward, it became the thesis of the experts that the pitch softened the fortitude of the Royals and paved the way for Phillies victories in the final two games of the Series.

Both players later denied that claim. Eventually, the issue was laid to rest. More than one decade later, however, Noles and Brett were scheduled to appear together at a Phillies function for fans.

"We didn't know each other, and hadn't seen each other since the Series," Noles said. "I was a little nervous about how it would go. I didn't quite know what to expect."

It didn't take long to resolve the uncertainty. When Brett arrived at the location that he would share with Noles, the jocular ex-third baseman had a baseball taped to each side of his face.

Fear of Flying

Flying is a fact of life for professional athletes. It's part of the business. It comes with the job.

That's not to say that all athletes enjoy flying. Some hate it. Phillies relief pitcher Ron Reed was deathly afraid of flying.

The Phillies were winging home from a road trip when their flight encountered a terrific storm. The plane bobbed around, loose articles fell out of the overhead racks.

Assume the position, Reed was told.

"What happens next?" he asked.

"Kiss your ass goodbye," came the reply.

Hail to the Chief

The Phillies got more than their money's worth when they signed Pete Rose. With his fire and spirit, Charley Hustle was the guy who lit the fuse on two Phils teams that went to the World Series.

Although he spent just five years with the Phillies, Rose reached one of the highest milestones of his 24-year career while playing in Philadelphia. In 1981, Rose tied Stan Musial's National League record for most hits in a career. The following day, major league players went on what the suits euphemistically call a work stoppage but what we working stiffs call a strike. When the strike ended 60 days later, play resumed, and in the first game back, Rose singled to break Musial's mark.

After the game, the Phillies held a press conference.

"I guess you're having the president call me," Rose said to public relations director Larry Shenk.

"The president will call if there's no crisis," Shenk replied.

The anticipated conversation was to be sent out over a loudspeaker. After being disconnected twice, President Ronald Reagan finally got through to congratulate the man who would later become baseball's all-time hit leader. The voice from the West Wing came through clearly.

"Pete, this is President Reagan."

"Hey, how you doin'?" Rose responded.

On his special night, even a call from the president didn't faze Pete Rose.
Courtesy of Rich Westcott

◆ ◆ ◆

Ballplayers are often the recipients of special gifts from fans. Once, a fan brought an 18-pound lobster to the clubhouse to give to Rose.

"It's not going to shit in my Bentley, is it?" Rose inquired, as the hearty crustacean crawled around the clubhouse floor.

◆ ◆ ◆

The Phillies lost the final game of the 1983 World Series 5-0 to the Baltimore Orioles. Eddie Murray led the way for the Birds, slugging two home runs, the second being a titanic blast into the upper deck in right field at Veterans Stadium.

"That ball," said Rose, "would have been a home run in Grand Canyon."

Bearing the Burden

In December 1982, the Phillies made one of their most controversial trades of the era. They swapped Manny Trillo, the MVP of the 1980 LCS and arguably the best-fielding second baseman the Phillies ever had; highly promising youngster Julio Franco, who is still playing after all these years; and three other players of reasonable merit (outfielder George Vukovich, pitcher Jay Baller, and catcher Jerry Willard) to the Cleveland Indians for outfielder Von Hayes.

Hayes, a slender slugger who was unfairly and imprecisely called the next Ted Williams, never really fulfilled what seemed to be his enormous potential, although he was not without some meritorious seasons. He once hit two home runs—one a grand slam—in the first inning in a 26-7 Phillies rout of the New York Mets. Throughout his career in Philadelphia, though, the likeable Hayes carried an unflattering label that stuck to him like peanut butter sticks to crackers. He was called "Five for One."

Room at the Top

The Phillies are one of the few teams—if not the only one—ever to fire a manager while the club was in first place. In 1983, Pat Corrales was replaced as manager after the 85th game. At the time, the Phils held the East Division lead with a 43-42 record.

General manager Paul Owens wielded the ax because he didn't like the way the multitalented Phillies—a team with four (it should be five) future Hall of Famers—were going about their business.

Owens put himself in charge, and the team went on to win the National League pennant.

It was the second time that Owens had stepped from the front office to the dugout. In 1972, he named himself as Frank Lucchesi's replacement so that he could get a firsthand look at the playing personnel.

The Phillies set a club record in the 1980s by employing seven different managers. Along with Owens and Corrales, the reins of the team were also handled by Dallas Green, John Felske, Lee Elia, interim pilot John Vukovich, and Nick Leyva.

Good Genes

The pitching capabilities of Steve Carlton were legendary. The superb southpaw was as dominating as any pitcher of his era and undoubtedly was one of the most unhittable hurlers of any era. It was so hard to apply a bat to one of Carlton's pitches that the renowned Pittsburgh Pirates slugger Willie Stargell once said, "Hitting him was like trying to drink coffee with a fork."

Carlton was also a legend in other ways. For one, his fanatical fitness regimen was superhuman. Lefty would walk back and forth in a four-foot-by-12-foot box in rice three feet deep. He could do 1,100 sit-ups at a time with 15-pound weights strapped to each wrist and each ankle. He even worked out for up to one and one-half hours after pitching in a game.

No less an authority than Carlton's conditioning guru (and that of a number of other Phillies players), the fabled John (Gus) Hoefling, said about the hurler, "Whoever put that man together genetically did one helluva job."

Traveling Incognito

When the Phillies won the National League pennant in 1983, it was a foregone conclusion who would be the club's starting pitcher against the Baltimore Orioles in the first game of the World Series. John Denny, who else?

Denny had won the NL's Cy Young Award that year, posting a 19-6 record, by far the best mark of his career. Prior to that, the former St. Louis Cardinals and Cleveland Indians hurler had never won more than 14 games in a season.

To say the least, Denny was an unusual character. Deeply religious, he was a practitioner of martial arts, and he refused to discuss his Cy Young Award at spring training the following spring. And he almost missed his first World Series assignment.

The first game was played in Baltimore, and the Phillies were staying at a downtown hotel. When Denny emerged from his room to board the team bus to Memorial Stadium, he discovered that it had already left. A hotel clerk, however, came to John's rescue. Pointing to a double-decker bus parked in front of the hotel, he told Denny that it was going to the ballpark. Denny could hitch a ride.

As fate would have it, the bus was filled with Orioles fans. Undaunted, Denny hopped aboard, climbed to the top deck, and rode to the park. The unsuspecting fans never knew who he was. Maybe if they had, Denny might not have pitched the Phils to their only win of the Series.

Unfamiliar Territory

Of the legions of young players who come to the big leagues with what seems to be limitless potential, Jeff Stone was one who fit the mold perfectly. He could hit, and oh man, could he run. Stoney stole 94 bases in the minors one year. That was nothing compared with the 123 he had swiped the year before.

Stone was the nicest guy you'd ever want to meet. He was a farm boy from Missouri, and when he was signed, the scout had to walk the last quarter-mile to his house. Stoney was about as friendly as your uncle's Labrador Retriever. He was also about as naïve as a groundhog.

But he had an inquisitive mind. While playing winter ball in Venezuela one year, he asked if it was the same moon there as they had in Missouri. That was about the time he left his television set

John Denny rode to the ballpark with a bus full of fans.
Photo courtesy of the Philadelphia Phillies

in Venezuela, saying he had no use for it back in the States. When asked why, he replied, "They only talk Spanish on it."

When a Phillies team bus traveling from the club's downtown hotel to Wrigley Field passed Lake Michigan, Stone was curious. "Is that the Atlantic or the Pacific Ocean?" he wanted to know. One time, Jeff was asked if he'd like a shrimp cocktail. "No thanks," he said. "I don't drink."

A New Hairdo

With Mike Schmidt, playing baseball was serious business. The introspective slugger was a keen student of the game, and he brought a workmanlike attitude to the ballpark. There was little room for merriment. Pranks and small talk were not part of his bag.

That is not to say that Schmidt was humorless. Far from it. When he let his hair down, Schmidt could be quite witty.

One night, allowing his sense of humor to surface, Schmidt let his hair way down. Well, sort of, anyway.

"I had had a pretty rough time the night before," he said. "The fans were really getting on me."

So Mike decided to have a little fun.

Teammate Larry Andersen had a collection of wigs. One wig had long, straight black hair, the kind you see kids wearing with their witch costumes on Halloween. Schmidt borrowed the wig, and as a playful way of hiding from the fans, wore it onto the field during infield practice.

Imagine the sight of the stoic slugger wearing a long-haired wig. The fans roared with laughter. They were seeing a side of Schmidt that they had seldom seen before. It turned them right around. And they gave him a standing ovation.

There were no shrimp cocktails for Jeff Stone. *Photo courtesy of the Philadelphia Phillies*

Masks and Wigs

Larry Andersen had a substantial collection of wigs and rubber face masks. The relief pitcher's inventory numbered 12 to 14 at its peak and even included a rubber likeness of Paul Owens.

How did the collection begin?

"My first one was a conehead," the current Phillies color analyst said. "I saw Sparky Lyle with one. It cracked me up. That got me started."

Andersen wore his cranial accoutrements around the clubhouse and sometimes on the field before games. He wore his Owens mask around the clubhouse after the Phillies clinched the pennant in 1983. Andersen kept most of the collection in his locker. It made for an interesting contrast—masks and wigs mixed in with spikes and gloves.

Putting on an Act

It was a Sunday afternoon, and a large crowd had gathered at Veterans Stadium to watch a Phillies game. At the time, Lee Elia was the team's manager. Elia was a rarity among Phillies skippers because he was one of only three Philadelphia natives who had piloted his hometown club.

In the midst of the game, a Phillies batter smoked a line drive down the third base line. Umpire Frank Pulli called it a foul ball. That brought Elia steaming out of the dugout.

"It was a foul ball," Pulli asserted.

Elia disagreed. Soon, he was engaged in a heated argument with Pulli. Heads bobbed, fingers were pointed; all of the sudden what had begun as a little discussion had escalated into a full-scale battle of words. When Elia fired his hat to the ground, he was ejected.

After the game, Pulli was asked for his version of the episode. (It's important to note here that he and Elia were good friends.) Pulli said that when Elia roared out of the dugout, he said, "What's wrong, Lee?"

Elia replied, "Frank, they're all over my ass upstairs [in the Phillies front office]. They say I'm not emotional. I'm supposed to be emotional, but they say I never do anything. So, I gotta go. Frank, you gotta throw me out."

Pulli said, "OK, if we're going to do that, let's make it a good one."

And they did.

The guy with the fancy hairdo is really reliever Larry Andersen.
Courtesy of Rich Westcott

Do Not Disturb

No hitter was ever born who relished the task of trudging to the plate to face Nolan Ryan. Especially if he batted from the right side.

The Hall of Fame pitcher with fastballs as quick as laser beams didn't strike out more than 5,700 batters and hurl the staggering total of seven no-hitters because he was a soft touch. No indeed. Ryan was as tough a pitcher as any batter ever faced. And certainly nobody ever wanted to make him mad.

Glenn Wilson knew this. The Phillies' strong-armed right fielder had faced Ryan many times—never with much success—

and he was fully aware that the big right-hander not only had a good arm, he also had a good memory.

During a game in the mid-1980s, though, Wilson had gotten lucky. He leaned into a Ryan fastball and poked it clear over the center field wall at Veterans Stadium. Despite the prodigious blast, Wilson wanted to stay low key.

"I ran around the bases as fast as I could," he said. "When I got to third base, I put my hands over the back of my jersey so he couldn't see my number. I got back to the bench, and the players all wanted to high-five me. I told them, 'Hurry up and sit down. I don't what him to know who hit that ball.'"

"That's how scared I was of Nolan Ryan," Wilson added. "I was never going to show that man up."

Pleading Innocent

One thing can be said about Kevin Gross: He was never lacking in the creativity department. Gross was a talented artist whose paintings were good enough to be sold at flattering prices. He also sculpted some pretty good games on the mound, including three Phillies seasons in double figures, plus a no-hitter after he left the Phils.

One time, though, Gross let his creative juices get the best of him. In a game in 1987 against the Chicago Cubs, plate umpire John Kibler had a sneaking suspicion that something was amiss. He wandered out to the mound, and upon checking Gross's glove, found a piece of sandpaper glued to the heel of the mitt. Naturally, Gross was ejected.

The pitcher was shocked. He didn't doctor balls, he claimed. And none of the balls he threw was scuffed, he insisted. "I played around with [the sandpaper] on the sidelines between starts, but it was just there in case I ever wanted to use it," Gross said. Whatever the case, Gross's fertile imagination was not appreciated. The baseball gods suspended him for 10 days.

No-Hit Pitchers

By no means have the Phillies had a corner on the market for pitchers who couldn't hit. But they've certainly had their share of them.

Bob Buhl was a notorious nonhitter. He pitched briefly for the Phils in the 1960s before retiring with a lifetime batting average of .089 in 15 seasons. Larry Andersen was another bashless basher. Although as a reliever he didn't come to the plate often, he got five hits—over a 17-year period—ending his career with a .132 average. Another fireman, Kent Tekulve, hit .083 in 16 years.

Then there was Don Carman. He went zero for his first 48 at-bats before finally managing to enjoy the rarity of a base hit in 1987. In 10 years on the mound, dangerous Don smoked the old pill for a .057 average.

Tuning Out

Michael (Mike) Jackson was a good one who got away. A promising young reliever, Jackson was part of an addlebrained trade in which the Phillies sent him and Glenn Wilson to the Seattle Mariners for Phil Bradley. Jackson went on to become one of the top firemen in the big leagues, and 15 years later he was still an effective bullpenner.

Jackson was often compared to the singer of the same name. "People used to tell me I look like Michael Jackson," he said. "Well, I don't sing like Michael Jackson. I don't even care for his music."

No Introduction Necessary

The Phillies roster has not always benefited from brilliant trades. In fact, there are some who've worn red pinstripes who really should have been wearing red faces. Their presence was that embarrassing.

Among many dim-witted trades of the late 1980s, the Phillies did, however, make a few good ones. One of the best was the deal that brought John Kruk and Randy Ready to the Phils in exchange for Chris James.

Kruk turned into a folk hero in Philadelphia, carrying both a bat and a personality that made him a favorite of legions of local fans who aren't overly attracted to players who shave every day, wear suits, and carry briefcases. Along with his lack of sartorial splendor, Kruk never hit below .291 and four times hit above .300 during his nearly six seasons with the Phillies.

When Kruk was traded to the Phils, he arrived at the ballpark and was greeted by a man whom he didn't know.

"Hi, I'm Bill Giles," the Phillies president said.

"Hi, I'm John Kruk, the new left fielder," came the reply.

Chapter 9

One Moment of Glory

1990-1999

Gypsies, Tramps, and Thieves

T he 1993 Phillies featured a band of players of outstanding talent and unusual behavior. No ordinary, dull, self-serving robots were these guys. Quite to the contrary, this was a group of intense but often playful jesters, who were a throwback to a much earlier era and who found immense pleasure in each other's company.

"Gypsies, tramps, and thieves," their leader Darren Daulton called them.

"We're a throwback, all right," John Kruk said. "Thrown back by other organizations."

"We lead the league in characters," Terry Mulholland added.

Some called the clubhouse a "nuthouse." Mitch Williams said it was populated by "a bunch of misfits." When the Phillies arrived in Atlanta, a newspaper warned residents to "hide the women and children." A Toronto rag reported that the Phils were "a motley crew of hairy, beer-soused brutes." The team was described as being "long-haired, slack-jawed, pot-bellied, and snarly-lipped."

To all this, burly outfielder Pete Incaviglia had a simple retort: "This ain't no ******* beauty show," he roared. "It's baseball. All that other stuff don't mean a thing."

The team was noted for its Macho Row, a section in the back of the clubhouse where the head honchos roosted. Daulton presided from a lounge chair crammed into his locker. Along with Kruk, the primary members of this august body included Lenny Dykstra, Dave Hollins, Williams, and Incaviglia.

Some of the descriptions of the Phillies were true. But to Philadelphians, the team was a popular collection of outcasts that appealed strongly to the city's often churlish fans. The 1993 Phillies, some of them socially challenged and many arriving in clever trades by general manager Lee Thomas, won the National League pennant. But to get to that point, the team, managed by Jim Fregosi, had to overcome a lackluster early part of the decade.

Even in 1992, the Phils finished last in the East Division. They went from the bottom to the top the following year, beating the vaunted Atlanta Braves in the league championship series. Curt Schilling led a talented pitching staff that advanced to the World Series as a decided underdog. The Phils, however, pressed the Toronto Blue Jays to six games before Williams threw the ill-fated ninth-inning home run pitch to Joe Carter.

The blow burst the Phillies' bubble. The team soon thereafter started to break up, and it would not have another winning season until 2001, which at that point gave it two seasons above .500 in 15 years.

Prime Time

Baseball is a sport that every now and then exhibits a keen sense of humor. It is a sport that fortunately does not have an iron-clad rule to take itself seriously.

A little humor surfaced after Tommy Greene pitched a no-hitter against the Montreal Expos in 1991. Greene was a sometimes outstanding hurler for the Phillies from 1990 to 1995 and was the proprietor of a 16-4 record in 1993.

But his most prominent game was the no-hitter pitched in Montreal. After the game, while Greene was being showered with beer and champagne, a call came into the clubhouse. Greene was told it was from the Prime Minister of Canada. Tommy excitedly rushed to the phone. There he learned that the caller was really a 17-year-old clubhouse boy that some of Greene's teammates talked into staging the ruse.

Missed Opportunity

Unassisted triple plays are one of the most uncommon occurrences in baseball. They almost never happen. In the Phillies' case, the rare feat has happened only once in the history of the franchise.

Second baseman Randy Ready had the chance in 1991 to become the first Phillies player to appear on such a highly select list, but he blew it. Randy snared a line drive off the bat of the San Diego Padres' Tony Gwynn, then tagged second base. All he had to do next was to tag the runner (coming from first base) who was right in front of him. But Ready absentmindedly threw to first, where Ricky Jordan recorded the third out.

So much for an unassisted triple play. The Phillies finally got one the following season when second baseman Mickey Morandini made the right plays on a liner by Jeff King of the Pittsburgh Pirates.

The Alpha Man

There are team leaders. And then there are team leaders. Some offer merely lip service. Some lead by example. Some step to the front of the pack and take over by the sheer force of their personalities.

Darren Daulton was the latter—and then some. He was the perfect definition of a team leader. The consummate pro, highly

No doubt about it, Darren Daulton ran the show. *Photo by Alan Kravetz*

respected, he set the tone—in spirit, with his presence, and by example. If he was in a wolf pack, he'd be the alpha wolf. If he was in the army, he'd be the general. Daulton is the guy who made the clock tick for the Phillies of the 1990s.

"He's like E.F. Hutton," said pitcher Larry Andersen. "When he speaks, everybody listens. It's like he's the Godfather, and we're all a bunch of thugs."

There was nothing halfway about Daulton, who his teammates called "Dutch." He always gave all he had. And he was not satisfied with mediocrity. Once, after watching a video of himself striking out, he was so disgusted that he socked a wall and broke his hand.

Daulton was a downright fine catcher and an excellent hitter. He was a stabilizing force behind the plate, a guy who handled pitches as well as he handled pitchers. In 1992, he led the National League in RBI with 109, making him only the fourth catcher in major league history to win an RBI crown. Over a two-year period of 1992-1993, he drove in 214 runs and collected 51 home runs.

Possessing matinee-idol good looks and a physique like a Greek god, Daulton, more than anybody, was the unchallenged king of the 1990s Phillies.

"There's no doubt in my mind that he has become the premier catcher in baseball," general manager Lee Thomas said in 1993. "Defensively, calling games, producing with the bat, you name it, he does it for us."

House of Dreams

There's nothing duller for baseball players than a long bus ride in spring training. Sometimes, however, a little comedy can liven up the trip.

The Phillies were on their way back to Clearwater after an exhibition game, and some of the fun lovers were in the back of the bus partaking of a few beverages. Darren Daulton had just signed a contract of substantial proportions, and some of his busmates were discussing the catcher's good (actually, it was very good) fortune.

"You know what you need to do, Dutch?" John Kruk said. "You need to build a big mansion, and we'll all live in it, party, have a good time, and play ball."

From another seat in the back of the bus came the voice of Pete Incaviglia.

"If you build it," he said, "we will come."

Numbers Game

After pitcher Tyler Green made the 1993 Phillies out of spring training, there was some question about what number he would wear. At the same time, reliever Mitch Williams had expressed an interest in wearing number 99, but equipment and clubhouse manager Frank Coppenbarger was against it.

Finally, Coppenbarger told Williams that if he got general manager Lee Thomas's approval, he would give him number 99. He would then give Williams's old number 28 to Green. Thomas consented, but before the switch was made, the guys decided to have some fun at the expense of coach John Vukovich.

Vukovich was very particular about his number 18, which he had worn throughout his career as a player and coach. The plot was to tell Vukovich that Green's agent had called and insisted that Green wear 18, and that Thomas had authorized the request.

Coppenbarger called Vukovich into his office to inform him of the change. "Vuke hit the ceiling," Coppenbarger said. "He ranted and raved for 15 minutes, then he went out into the clubhouse and kicked trunks, trash cans, everything in sight."

Manager Jim Fregosi, who was in on the gag, told Vukovich, "There's no way I'm going to let this happen. I'll go upstairs and straighten this out."

"No, no," Vukovich pleaded, "don't do that."

Finally, the beleaguered coach was told the truth. He was not happy to learn he had been the victim of a clubhouse prank.

Lenny Dykstra was once compared to a mosquito. *Photo by Alan Kravetz*

Get Out the Bug Spray

While he lasted, Lenny Dykstra was one of the spark plugs that made the Phillies engine go. The spunky center fielder hit above .300 three times for the Phils during the early 1990s. He played a major role in the club's 1993 trip to the World Series.

Unfortunately, injuries and other problems plagued Dykstra throughout much of his career, and he never quite reached the level he or others thought he would. He lost $78,000 in card games and golf matches in the late 1980s. In 1991, he was seriously injured after his Mercedes went out of control and hit a tree on a country road while returning from a bachelor party for John Kruk. Passenger Darren Daulton was also hurt in the crash.

Hard as it may be to believe, Dykstra had only three full seasons with the Phillies. At least parts of five other years were missed because of injuries. He endured surgery six different times and suffered at least eight broken bones, including his collarbone twice. Overall, "The Dude" visited the disabled list 10 times.

Dykstra was a cocky, scrappy, feisty, sometimes arrogant little guy who chewed tobacco, spat often, and didn't give much of a hoot what anybody else thought about him.

"He's like a mosquito when you're outdoors," Phils manager Nick Leyva said. "You're always waiting for him to bite you."

Happy Hour

Nobody ever accused Danny Jackson of having a reserved personality. No way. The Phillies pitcher was your classic left-hander: a free spirit, to say the least.

Jackson, who was often surly and once said he won a game because he was motivated to "stick it up the media's ass," played a key role in the Phillies' drive to the 1993 National League pennant. He won 12 games, and with better offensive support could have won four or five more. After some of his wins, Jackson had an unusual way of celebrating. Once, he smashed a soda can on his head. Naturally, he put a gash in his skull.

One of Jackson's more prominent feats was to rip off his shirt and, doing an imitation of The Incredible Hulk, "pump it up." It was a strange sight to see. But it always got a rise out of his amused teammates.

He's No Astaire

Another postgame activity that followed a Phillies win in 1993 was the celebratory show staged by Todd Pratt. The team's reserve catcher would dance in the clubhouse to the tune of "Whoop, There It Is," a popular ditty that the Phillies more or less adopted that season as their theme song.

"It looked weird," said that noted observer of social mores, John Kruk. "He had no rhythm at all. He looked like a white guy trying to dance like a black guy. But he did it every time we won. Don't ask me why."

Sick Jokes

No player ever overcame a greater or more debilitating handicap that Jim Eisenreich. The gentlemanly outfielder suffered from Tourette's Syndrome, and although he had the illness under control by the time he reached the Phillies, he had previously missed nearly four seasons.

A quiet, gracious man, the gallant Eisenreich was a major player with the Phillies for four seasons, never hitting below .300, and one year pounding out a lofty .361. Eisenreich was popular with his teammates, but as ballplayers often do, they teased him about his affliction. John Kruk jokingly requested some of Eisey's medicine, saying he needed it to calm down. And Curt Schilling, when first told about Eisenreich's condition, said, "Compared to what most of us have on this team, that's like having a common cold."

The Good Humor Man

The best natural hitter on the Phillies of the 1990s was a slugging outfielder/first baseman who liked to play the role of a scruffy hick from the backwoods of West Virginia. Those who hung around John Kruk knew otherwise. Beneath that shaggy hair and baggy uniform resided a sharp, witty, nimble brain that was far removed from the country bumpkin he often portrayed.

Kruk was the kind of guy who looked like he couldn't hit a baseball if you handed it to him. Yet, he never hit less than .291 in his six seasons with the Phillies, four times going over .300. No Phillies hitter of the 1990s was as consistent or as dependable as Kruk.

He also had his quirks. Often, he chewed 20 sticks of gum at once, saying it helped him to relieve tension. Once, after a game, he played whiffleball in the clubhouse until 7 a.m. with members of the Phillies' ground crew. Thinking he didn't have to play the next game, Kruk claimed he pitched 30 or 40 innings. He took a short nap in the clubhouse, and when he awoke, he was so sore he

Don't accuse John Kruk of being an athlete. *Photo by Alan Kravetz*

could hardly move. That night, he was in the starting lineup after all. He laced three hits.

Away from the plate, Kruk had another side. He was the master of the one-liner, a comedian of the highest echelon. In a restaurant, where he was drinking beer, smoking, and enjoying a big dinner, Kruk was approached by a woman who recognized him. The woman berated him unmercifully, saying that no professional athlete should have that many bad habits.

"I ain't an athlete, lady," Kruk replied. "I'm a baseball player."

◆ ◆ ◆

When the Phillies won the National League pennant by beating the Atlanta Braves in a thrilling six-game National League Championship Series, the analysts quickly went to work. How, they wondered, could such a band of rogues with scant experience in the pressure-cooker of the playoffs go from worst to first while beating a team that was stuffed with star players and that was a regular visitor to the postseason merriment?

Kruk had the answer.

"[The Braves] were the most arrogant people in the world," he postulated. "But we didn't care who they were or what they thought. Our feeling was, they could just kiss our asses."

◆ ◆ ◆

The master of the artful quote, Kruk, who once appeared on the David Letterman show with a two-day-old beard and wearing a baseball cap, worn-out jeans, and a T-shirt promoting a rock band, was not fond of playing in Denver. "I couldn't play here," he said. "I wouldn't breathe. And if I can't breathe, I'm going to die. It's a nice city, but what the hell would you see of it when you're dead?"

The Morning After

Doubleheaders were once a highly popular attraction. But big league teams don't go for twin bills anymore. Unless there's a rained-out game that has to be made up, they're as shunned as a nine-inning pitcher. In this era of corporate ownership headed by devotees of the almighty bottom line, a doubleheader is thought to produce fewer fans—and hence fewer dollars—than two games played on separate days.

That unfortunate logic notwithstanding, the dinosaur known as a doubleheader does occasionally rear its princely head. The Phillies had one of particular note during their hellion days of 1993.

Returning from a road trip, the Phils were scheduled to play—heaven forbid—two games in one night against the Padres. With an original crowd of 54,617 in attendance, the first game, slated to start at 4:35 p.m., experienced three rain delays totaling five hours and 44 minutes. (One with a fair degree of sanity might justifiably ask why such a game was not canceled.) The game was finally completed slightly after 1 a.m. with San Diego winning 5-2.

The second game began sharply at 1:26 a.m. It lasted 10 innings. As the game progressed, the miniscule crowd that had lingered miraculously expanded as fans with peculiar sleeping habits began flocking to the stadium to witness the history-making event. The end finally came when weak-hitting relief pitcher Mitch Williams, in his only at-bat of the season, lashed a single that drove in the run that gave the Phillies a 6-5 victory.

The clock said it was 4:40 a.m., the latest a major league game had ever finished. That was 12 hours and five minutes after the first game had started. Actual playing time totaled five hours and 46 minutes.

Five days later, the Phillies played another marathon. This time they went 20 innings to beat the Los Angeles Dodgers 7-6 in a game that took six hours and 10 minutes to play. The game ended at 2:20 a.m.

Steer Clear of Mikey

It would be a gross understatement to say that Dave Hollins was intense. The Phillies' third baseman was so intense that you could almost see the fire billowing out of his mouth like an agitated dragon.

Hollins played baseball the way a surgeon operates on a patient. Total concentration. Single-minded, almost to a fault. He came to the Phillies as a nobody and willed himself into being a fine hitter and a major part of the 1993 team.

Clubhouse banter held that Hollins was really two people. He was Dave, the enthusiastic, energetic, hustling player liked by all his teammates. Then there was Dave's evil twin Mikey, the cursing, hot-tempered, brooding manic, who could erupt into a bad mood as quickly as an umpire could say, "Strike three."

Mikey (Hollins's middle name is Michael) could become so highly inflamed that Larry Bowa, then a Phillies coach, said, "If you had 25 guys on the team like Hollins, they would have all killed each other by the third week of the season."

Beer Men

After a long road trip to a spring training exhibition game, the Phillies bus returned to Clearwater, whereupon the clubhouse men quickly set about unloading the myriad bags of equipment. While that was going on, the players retired to the locker room to drink a few beers. The trouble was all the beer had been consumed during the bus ride.

So the thirsty players suggested that clubhouse assistant Phil Sheridan run to a nearby store to buy some beer. But clubhouse and equipment manager Frank Coppenbarger demurred, claiming that he couldn't release one of his men because there was too much work to do and he couldn't lose the time or the manpower. Pitcher Larry Andersen asked Coppenbarger what Sheridan had to do.

"Well," Coppenbarger said, "right now, all that catching gear and all those batting helmets have to be cleaned and put away."

Andersen replied, "If I do the work, will you let him go get the beer?"

Finally, Coppenbarger relented. And a few minutes later, Andersen, with towel in hand, was busy cleaning the mud and crud off the equipment while Sheridan went to purchase the players' beverage of choice.

To Have or Not to Have

During the 1990s, the Phillies had no better pitcher than Curt Schilling. The big right-hander had gone through unsuccessful stints—would you believe, mostly as a reliever?—with three major league clubs before the Phillies rescued him and had the good sense to put him in the starting rotation.

Finally where he should have been all along, Schilling, who whenever he pitched always left a ticket for his deceased father as a way of acknowledging his dad's profound influence on his life, blossomed into a standout moundsman. He won 101 games for Phillies clubs that were—with one exception—not exactly terrors. That is not to say, though, that Schill was always effective.

One day, the fireballing hurler was getting hit early in the game by a heavy barrage of enemy batpower. Catcher Darren Daulton thought it was time for a chat.

He strolled out to the mound and said, "Schilling, you don't have shit today. So we're going to have to trick these guys."

At about that point, the Phils' highly regarded pitching coach, Johnny Podres, ambled out to the mound, and in his best imitation of Dale Carnegie, told Schilling, "You've got great stuff. Just keep firing. You're looking good."

Suitably confused, Schilling shook his head and peered quizzically at Daulton.

"Which is it?" he asked.

"You ain't got shit," Daulton answered.

Dealing

The Phillies franchise is, of course, not entirely devoid of low points. What would you expect from a team that's finished in last place more than any other club in the history of baseball?

Possibly the lowest point for the Phillies—maybe even outranking the great collapse of 1964—occurred on the last pitch of 1993 when Mitch Williams delivered a home run ball to Joe Carter in the bottom of the ninth in the sixth game of the World

Curt Schilling was the recipient of some mixed signals. *Photo by Alan Kravetz*

Series. The blast gave the Toronto Blue Jays an 8-6 victory and the World Series.

Manager Jim Fregosi was criticized long and loud for using the worn-out Williams in that situation. And "Wild Thing" was angrily skewered for serving such a disastrous pitch. In the aftermath, his house was vandalized, and his life was threatened by mindless social misfits.

Williams, who had done yeoman duty during the season, saving 43 games, which at the time was a club record, and winning two and saving two more in the league championship series with Atlanta, didn't run and hide after the game like a lot of big-game goats would have done. Much to his credit, he stood by his locker, answering wave after wave of questions from the inquisitive media horde.

"The one thing that bothers me is that I let my teammates down," he said bravely. "They busted their butts all year long, and I let them down. I threw the pitch that cost us the World Series. But I can carry that burden. It's my job to deal with it."

A few months later, the burden that Williams shouldered in Philadelphia was lifted. He was dealt to the Houston Astros.

Quick Exit

It's doubtful that anyone ever made a more bizarre major league debut than Andy Carter. A big, strong pitcher, Carter spent parts of two seasons in the mid-1990s working out of the Phillies' bullpen.

Carter was a local guy, and he probably had some hometown fans in the stands when he entered his first big league game in 1994. Only trouble was, he didn't last long enough to give the hometown folks much to cheer about.

Upon entering a game against San Diego, Carter hit two of the first three batters he faced. Umpire Jim Quick quickly ejected him. League rules, you know.

Play Ball

During the strike of 1994 that extended into 1995, various Phillies players tried to keep in shape while they were locked out of their regular spring training camp by working out at several fields in the Clearwater area. One day, however, some of them decided that they'd had enough of dried-out dirt fields that resembled small deserts. So they headed for Jack Russell Stadium, where the club regularly trained.

Naturally, the place was locked when Curt Schilling, Tommy Greene, and Dave Hollins arrived. Undeterred, the trio left their cars in a far corner of the parking lot, grabbed their equipment, and sneaked onto the practice field like little kids who'd just walked off with the cookie jar. Consider the absurdity of high-priced big leaguers having to sneak onto a field so that they could play a little baseball.

The session continued for about one and one-half hours. It was only a matter of time before club president Bill Giles learned about the caper. He told Jayson Stark of *The Philadelphia Inquirer* that he was happy his players were working out. "But I think they should work out on their own somewhere else," he said.

Seldom without an opinion, Schilling offered his view. "It's kind of hilarious when you think about it—trying to be secretive about playing baseball," he said to Stark. "I mean, it's not like national security is involved."

Rookie in Drag

Hazing may be something that's connected with pledging to a fraternity, but it's also a practice that takes place in baseball. The veterans initiate the rookies at some point during the season.

The hazing process often takes place on the last day of a road trip. During the away game, a veteran player enters the rookie's locker and heists and hides his street clothes. He replaces them with some outrageous garb, usually women's clothes, a Batman costume, or some other outlandish kind of attire. Naturally, when

As Scott Rolen learned, rookie hazing can be brutal. *Photo by Alan Kravetz*

the player returns to the clubhouse after the game, he finds that he has nothing else to wear unless he wants to leave the ballpark dressed in his uniform.

Often, the annual ritual takes an unexpected twist—at least for the hazee. Such was the case in 1997 when, with several other freshmen, Scott Rolen was a victim of some creative hazing on his way to becoming National League Rookie of the Year.

Rolen arrived unsuspectingly at his locker after a game in Chicago only to find that his clothes had disappeared from his locker. A pink halter top and a poodle skirt were left in place of his pants and shirt.

The rookie third baseman had no choice but to put on the clothes. It so happened that, because he lived not too far from Chicago, Rolen's parents, his future wife and her friends, other relatives, and many of his old buddies, including his high school coach, had attended the game. Rolen was supposed to meet this large entourage after the game at the gate in right field where players from the visiting team boarded their bus.

To the utter shock of the Rolen group, Scott emerged from the corridor that connected the clubhouse and the gate wearing his womanly garments. If that wasn't bad enough, though, chief prankster Rex Hudler had arranged for the bus to be relocated to a spot behind the home plate entrance. Thus, Rolen and the other rookies had to walk the long block from where the bus was supposed to be to where it was.

Not only was Rolen totally embarrassed, Cubs fans, a goodly number of whom were suffering from the consumption of too many brewery products, took pictures and gave him a razzing like he'd never heard before or since.

A Brush with the Law

There are many forms of hazing. Some occured when a team goes through customs on its way to Canada. Another routinely took place in Chicago on the trip between the downtown hotel and Wrigley Field. Until the practice was halted by Major League

Baseball at the request of the city of Chicago, the ritual was performed by every team in the National League.

Along the route to the ballpark resides a statue of a general on a horse. It sits on a pedestal about eight feet high with the horse, rearing back on its hind legs, obviously reaching well above the pedestal.

For many years, rookies from NL teams were required to sneak out during the night and paint the horse's testicles in team colors. Ordinarily, one player had to stand on another's shoulders to reach the designated target. Using spray paint, players often added their numbers or initials to the artwork. The veterans inspected the quality of the work the next day as their bus passed the statue.

Once, in a prearranged scheme after the Phillies' bus arrived at Wrigley Field, two Chicago policemen entered the clubhouse looking for the culprits who had applied paint to the horse's privates. Someone gave them the names of the rookies involved. The cops then conferred with manager Terry Francona. In a rare outburst, Francona, who was part of the prank, emerged from his office and berated his minions unmercifully.

Then the police informed the players that anybody who defaced public property was subject to arrest. Scared rookies squirmed. Several were reduced practically to tears when the lawmen told them to get out of their uniforms and prepare for a trip to the police station.

"I'm from Chicago and my mom and dad will be so upset with me. I'm so embarrassed," bawled one rookie suspect.

The whole scheme was a big production. The cops screamed at the rookies. The veterans had trouble stifling guffaws. Francona continued his tirade. And finally, the rookies were hauled out of the clubhouse, ostensibly to be carted off to jail.

One of them was relief pitcher Wayne Gomes. While playing at Scranton/Wilkes-Barre the year before, Gomes had been given a badge by local police that declared him an honorary deputy.

"If you ever get into a jam," Gomes was told, "show your badge and you might get a break."

Showing no lack of memory, Gomes reached into his bag, pulled out the badge, and showed it to the cops.

"We don't honor any country hillbilly badge like that," one cop screeched, flinging the badge back at Gomes. "Get in the car."

As they got outside and approached a waiting police car, the officers exposed the trick. At that point, as was always the case, the color began returning to the faces of the victims. Of course, as always, they reappeared in the clubhouse insisting to their teammates that they hadn't been the least bit scared.

Flawless Fielder

Rare is the baseball player these days who takes special pride in his defense. For most players, the emphasis is on offense. How many home runs have I hit lately?

A contrast to that breed was Rico Brogna, a masterful first baseman who might be the best at that position that the Phillies ever had. Only Eddie Waitkus, Bill White, Willie Montanez, Tommy Hutton, and Travis Lee could be mentioned in the same breath as Brogna.

The sure-handed Brogna played the bag like Grover Washington played the sax. Smoothly. Elegantly. With style and grace. Comparing Brogna to most other first basemen was like comparing cashmere to burlap.

During one stretch, Brogna made just 19 errors in 4,500 chances. He fielded .998 in 1998, making only three miscues all season. Brogna could hit, too. He drove in more than 100 runs two years in a row. In 1998, his 110 RBI were the most for a Phillies first baseman in 66 years.

But it was his defense of which Brogna was most proud.

"I simply enjoy playing defense," he said. "I love that part of the game. I take a lot of pride in playing good defense, and I've spent a lot of time working on it. But when you like what you're doing, all the work is easy."

Getting Lit Up

Any time a pitcher gets battered, there's a good chance that at least one thing's certain to happen. He'll have a rationale for his demise. Didn't have my good stuff. My arm hurt. I was hungover. My mother-in-law is visiting. It's a tried and true practice of pitchers to have a ready explanation when their mound offerings are flawed.

Mark Leiter, a pitcher who paid a brief visit to the Phillies in the late 1990s, got especially creative one day when his deliveries were not finding their way into fielders' gloves. Leiter had yielded six or seven runs early in the game and was on the verge of testing the hot water in the showers when he signaled that he wanted to discuss the situation with catcher Mike Lieberthal.

Lieberthal tromped out to the mound to hear his pitcher's tale of woe. It so happened that it was one of those rare afternoon games and the sun was shining through the stands behind home plate.

"I can't see your glove," Leiter said, pointing to the sun. Sure enough, when Lieberthal turned to face home plate, he saw that the sun was indeed shining brightly.

But the catcher really wasn't buying Leiter's excuse.

"I was trying to be as subtle as I could, but we had a different rationale," he said, hinting that there was really another reason the Phils' hurler was getting—excuse the pun—lit up. It had something to do with Leiter having nothing on the ball but his fingerprints.

Batting Binges

For some reason, the Phillies have been a team that often hits its home runs in clumps.

They can go a week without even a hint of a long ball, and then all of a sudden break into a barrage of homers.

One of the most recent times that four-baggers flew all over the lot was in 1999, when for the fourth time in club history, Phillies batters connected for three consecutive homers. The timely taps were delivered by Scott Rolen, Rico Brogna, and Ron Gant in the first inning of a game against the Cincinnati Reds at Veterans Stadium.

Just one year earlier, Phils sluggers had unloaded a club-record seven home runs in one game against the New York Mets. Rico Brogna, Bobby Estalella, and Kevin Sefcik each homered twice before Marlon Anderson set the record with a pinch-hit, seventh-inning homer in his first major league at-bat.

Going back a little bit, in 1985 Von Hayes bashed balls out of the park twice in the first inning as the Phils clobbered the Mets 26-7. One of Hayes's dingers was a grand slam. And in 1949 against the Reds, Phillies batters—Andy Seminick with two, and Del Ennis, Willie Jones, and Schoolboy Rowe with one apiece—all reached the fences in the same inning, tying a major league record.

A Losing Lesson

Over the years, baseball has come up with a variety of cliches about and definitions of winning. Curt Schilling, a devoted student of the game and its history, contributed this view:

"The toughest lesson I've ever had to learn—and also the most rewarding—is that losing is the only way to grasp the true meaning of winning."

Chapter 10

Back in the Race Again

2000-2005

Changes Make a Difference

As the 21st century began, there was hardly any reason to believe that the Phillies would be any different from their immediate predecessors. This was a team, after all, that by the end of 2000 had accumulated seven straight losing seasons. It hadn't come remotely close to making the playoffs. Indeed, there was no joy in Philsville.

What a difference a year makes! In 2001, the Phillies finished over .500 for only the second time since 1993—and the third time since 1986—and were in the race for a playoff spot until late in the season. And after barely winding up below .500 in 2002, the Phillies registered winning records in each of the next three years, a feat the team had not accomplished since the 1970s.

In 2005, the Phils, while posting the fourth-best record in the major leagues and the top record in the East Division since early July, went down to the final game of the season before getting eliminated from a playoff berth. Indicative of the way the season went, the Phillies had four players in the top 15 in the Most Valuable Player voting. Pat Burrell was seventh, Jimmy Rollins 11th, Chase Utley 13th, and Bobby Abreu 15th.

The key to the Phillies' renewed success was change. The ballpark changed. Managers changed. The lineup changed. The latter was punctuated by the emergence of several players as top-level performers and the signing of several major free agents.

Abreu ascended to the top layer of National League sluggers. Rollins moved into the upper echelon of NL shortstops. Utley gained a spot as one of the up-and-coming stars of the league. Burrell returned from a horrendous yearlong slump to become one of the circuit's top power hitters. And Ryan Howard quickly made a mark by winning Rookie of the Year honors.

All the while, key free agents were coming to town. First to come was Jim Thome. Then David Bell. He was followed by Jon Leiber. The Phils landed Billy Wagner in a trade. And the farm system delivered players such as Brett Myers, Ryan Madson, and Jason Michaels to go along with other home-grown products such as Rollins, Utley, Burrell, Howard, Mike Lieberthal, and Randy Wolf.

Some vital players departed. Prodded by various levels of dissatisfaction, Curt Schilling, Scott Rolen, and eventually Placido Polanco left town in trades that in the long run returned virtually nothing to the Phils. Polanco came in the Rolen deal, but no one swapped for those three players remains in Philadelphia.

On the bench, Terry Francona begat Larry Bowa who begat Charlie Manuel as the Phillies went from managers who were laid back to intense to laid back in their styles. And ultimately, Ed Wade gave way to Pat Gillick in a momentous switch in general managers. Somewhat ironically, Gillick was the general manager of the Toronto Blue Jays when they beat the Phils in the 1993 World Series.

No change in the early part of the 21st century was any bigger than the one in 2004 when the Phillies moved out of Veterans Stadium and into brand new Citizens Bank Park. After 33 years, the multipurpose Vet had become obsolete by today's sports standards. In its place came a venue that was created strictly for baseball, that was attractive and more luxurious, and that catered to the specific needs and desires of not only modern Major League Baseball teams and players, but of the current breed of fans.

Some 3,250,092 fans—a number that featured 44 sellouts, including 10 in a row—packed the park in what was an all-time Phillies attendance record. The park's one flaw—a left-field fence that was too close to home plate, thus yielding too many home runs—was addressed before the start of the 2006 season with the removal of several rows of bleacher seats.

Meanwhile, based on the team's performance during the first half of the new century's first decade, the Phillies had regained a place among the league's better teams. How permanent that would be remains to be seen.

Patriotic Pitcher

While he was with the Phillies, Nelson Figueroa wasn't particularly successful as a player. But the pitcher, who came in the trade for Curt Schilling, left an indelible mark in another way.

Following the tragedy of September 11, Figueroa, a native of Brooklyn, took it upon himself to design and market shirts that served as a poignant reminder of that horrible day. Using a baseball that was covered by the American flag as its centerpiece, the shirts carried words above and below the baseball. "For All The Victims And The Heroes," the top lines read. "United We Stand," it said on the bottom.

Asked what inspired his patriotic gesture, Figueroa, a graduate of Brandeis University, said, "It's something I wanted to do to help us remember all the people who were involved."

An astronomical number of shirts were sold. Proceeds were earmarked for the families of the victims.

Take Your Pick

When Scott Rolen decided that on the whole he would rather not be in Philadelphia, the Phillies were forced to make a trade with the St. Louis Cardinals. One of the players the Phils got for Rolen was aging reliever Mike Timlin.

Timlin had previously been with four major league teams since he first set foot in the big leagues in 1991, but according to public record, he was still in search of his first Cy Young Award. Yet, the pitcher was still an expert on the process of winning.

"Even though we've been winning since I've been here," Timlin told Bob Brookover of *The Philadelphia Inquirer*, "these guys don't seem like they have a lot of fun winning. When you win, you should have fun."

Feisty manager Larry Bowa was not amused.

"Do you want to have fun or do you want to come in last?" the skipper asked.

Time to Get a Bath

The Phillie Phanatic has been causing mayhem at Veterans Stadium and elsewhere since the peculiar animal was allegedly discovered on the Galapagos Islands in 1978. Since then, its good-humored antics have made it a particular favorite among fans and one of the most prominent mascots in sports.

The furry, green whatever-it-is, portrayed for its first 17 years by Dave Raymond and since 1995 by Tom Burgoyne, has its fun both on the field and off. But it is not always comical, as the Phanatic's long-running feud some years ago with then-Los Angeles Dodgers manager Tom Lasorda attests.

Sometimes, too, a stunt backfires. That happened on the night Scott Rolen made his first appearance at Veterans Stadium after his trade to the Cardinals. It was also the 25th anniversary of the death of Elvis Presley.

Appropriately, the Phanatic, who among other things is noted for his excessive body odor, was dressed in an Elvis costume. As he often does, he carried a tamper to smash a plastic hat that looks like the kind the opposition wears. As he went to apply the tamper to the hat near the Cardinals' dugout, third base coach Jose Oquendo tried to grab it. In the process he knocked over the Phanatic, who then proceeded to drench Oquendo with his water gun.

Oquendo retaliated by grabbing a cooler of ice water from the St. Louis dugout and dumping it over the Phanatic.

"In all the years I've been doing the Phanatic, I've never been that drenched," Burgoyne said.

The Wrong Brother

When the Phillies acquired Jeremy Giambi during the 2002 season in a trade with the Oakland Athletics, the deal added a proven power-hitter to the club's roster. But it also continued a long Phillies tradition of having the wrong brother.

Throughout their history, the Phils have made a habit of suiting up the lessor of two siblings. Having Jeremy Giambi instead of Jason was the latest example.

Over the years, Phillies uniforms have been worn by Mike Maddux instead of Greg. Ken Brett instead of George. Frank Torre instead of Joe. Rick Surhoff instead of B.J. Mark Leiter instead of Al. And way back, the Phils had Vince DiMaggio instead of Joe or Dom. Harry Walker (so he did win a batting title) instead of Dixie. Emil Meusel instead of Bob. And Harry Coveleski instead of Stan.

All has not been lost, however. On the plus side, Phils players have included Ed Delahanty instead of any one of his four ball-playing brothers. Granny Hamner instead of Garvin. And Dick Allen instead of Ron or Hank.

Keep It Down

In the midst of its swan song, baseball in Montreal became only slightly more popular than snowmobiling in Florida. Few fans followed the Expos, and even fewer attended their games.

One Phillies-Expos game in 2002 drew the staggering total of 2,134 fans. Considering that the ballpark holds more than 46,000, that's like having one car an hour drive the Schuylkill Expressway.

After the game, winning pitcher Randy Wolf noted how little noise there was in the stands.

"If there had been a cricket in the dugout," he said about the silence, "you would have been able to hear it."

Letter to the Editor

After the end of the 2002 season, pitcher Vicente Padilla did one of the most astounding things ever to be connected with professional sports. He wrote a letter to a newspaper, thanking the Phillies and their fans for supporting him throughout the season.

Is that incredible, or what? A professional athlete thanking anybody for anything would be earth-shattering news. But to make a public statement in a newspaper? Absolutely astonishing. It was enough to make a reader speechless for a month.

During the 2002 season, the young hurler, who had come to the Phillies as a reliever as part of the trade for Curt Schilling, emerged as one of the top chuckers on the staff. Although he barely spoke English—obviously, someone helped him pen his letter—he became a popular player among the rank-and-file Phils fans.

Padilla's sincere correspondence appeared in *The Philadelphia Inquirer*. In it, he thanked "the people of Philadelphia for welcoming him to their wonderful city." And he thanked the Phillies organization for the help it had given him. Professional sports should thank Padilla for such a noble undertaking.

An Impressive Debut

When Jim Thome signed as a free agent with the Phillies prior to the 2003 season, his arrival was greeted with as much excitement and enthusiasm as any athlete ever to come to Philadelphia. From his first visit on, Thome easily captured the fancy of local sports fans desperately in search of a hero.

Vicente Padilla authored a highly unusual letter. *Photo courtesy of the Philadelphia Phillies*

Thome's instant popularity was no surprise. Not only did he bring to town the credentials as one of the game's most productive power hitters—a commodity that was sorely needed in the Phillies' lineup—he was a hard-working, down-to-earth guy with good manners, an unassuming demeanor, and a total lack of the me-first, kiss my feet, showboat attitude so prevalent among today's high-priced prima donnas.

Thome provided an early glimpse of his makeup when he had a limo stop so he could jump out and shake hands with a group of electricians working on the Phillies' new ballpark. It continued when he was overcome with emotion while talking about his wife, Andrea, at his introductory press conference.

Here was a player, it became readily apparent, who was honest and sincere, a team player, a guy who signed autographs, talked to fans, and never shunned the media. Of course, his estimated six-year, $85-million contract was also an attention-getter.

Nothing, though, captured the spotlight any more than Thome's bat. Right from the start, it was clear that the big first baseman was going to be well worth the time and money the Phillies had invested in bringing him to Philadelphia.

Reporting to spring training in Clearwater early, Thome astounded onlookers by clubbing a batting practice pitch of manager Larry Bowa's that cleared the right field fence, and flew over a creek and some resident alligators, up over a high embankment, and out onto a major highway (Route 19). Although the blast was wind-aided, no one before had ever hit such a poke at the Phils' spring training base.

"The ball took a road trip," said Phillies adviser and former manager Dallas Green.

And Thome was just getting started. In his first Phillies at-bat in an exhibition game, he belted a home run. In his first at-bat of the season, he smacked a triple and then scored the club's first run of the campaign. In his first at-bat at the Phillies' home opener, he laced a two-run double.

Thome's awesome blasts continued throughout the season. At one point, he homered in three straight games. He had six two-

Jim Thome arrived in Philadelphia and let his bat do the talking.
Rich Pilling/Getty Images

home run games. He hit two-run homers in four straight games. He set a club record with 10 home runs in September. He hit the final home run at Veterans Stadium. And he led the National League in home runs with 47, the second-highest total in Phillies history.

It was, as even the most jaded observer had to admit, a dazzling season that had turned out exactly as had been expected.

All in the Family

Signing David Bell to a Phillies contract before the 2003 season not only gave the club a much-needed third baseman, it also gave the Phils another branch of a big league family tree.

In Bell's case, it's a three-generation tree. Grandfather Gus was a major league outfielder from 1950 to 1964, playing most notably with the Pittsburgh Pirates and Cincinnati Reds. Father Buddy played from 1972 to 1989, primarily as a third baseman with the Cleveland Indians and Texas Rangers, and also managed several big league teams. And David first came up in 1995 and spent most of his time with the Seattle Mariners before joining the Phillies.

In 2004, David hit for the cycle, only the eighth one in Phillies history. Gus also hit for the cycle—in 1951 against the Phillies at Shibe Park.

Only three families in major league history have sent three generations of players to the big leagues. One was the Hairstons, Sammy, Jerry, and Jerry Jr. Like the Bells, the other one has ties with the Phillies, too.

At the start of his 18-year career, Bob Boone was a catcher with the Phillies from 1972 to 1981. His father Ray (Ike) was a major league infielder from 1948 to 1960. Bob's sons Bret and Aaron have been manning infield posts in the bigs since the 1990s.

The Phillies have other noteworthy entries in the ancestral register. Ruben Amaro Sr. and Jr. are the only father-and-son duo to play with the Phils. A father, Tito Francona, played with the Phils and his son, Terry, managed the club. Eight sets of brothers, most recently Dennis and Dave Bennett in 1964, played with the

Phillies. And dad Bob and son Ruly Carpenter were both presidents of the team.

Worth the Wait

Nobody ever said there is no virtue in patience. Less than 24 hours after sitting for nearly 45 minutes on a curb at a gas station in the middle of nowhere waiting for a ride, Chase Utley crashed into the Phillies' record book.

He did it by making his first major league hit a grand slam home run. The April 24, 2003, blast at Veterans Stadium made Utley the third Phillies player to smack a grand slam for his first big league hit and just the sixth in major league history to do it.

Less than one day earlier, Utley had been a member of the Scranton/Wilkes-Barre Red Barons, the Phillies' Triple-A farm club. But when Phils infielder Placido Polanco joined the disabled list with an injured finger, Utley was summoned to take his place.

At the time, Utley was on the team bus headed for Ottawa. Red Barons manager Marc Bombard, riding in the front of the bus, was reached on his cell phone and advised of the move.

"The bus pulls over, and Bombard comes walking back," Utley said. "He told me, 'You just got called up to Philadelphia. You're going to have to get off the bus.' So I got off."

Utley was told to await a ride back to Scranton where he could pick up his clothes and car and head to Philadelphia. Only trouble was the bus was somewhere between the Pennsylvania–New York border, miles from anything except a gas station and an adjoining sandwich shop. Without even as much as a bite to eat, Utley plunked himself down on the curb and waited.

"I sat there about 45 minutes until one of the clubhouse guys from Scranton picked me up," Utley said later. "Sitting on a curb at a gas station is not exactly the way you envision waiting to get to the big leagues."

The next night, Utley, who had one at-bat in a brief appearance with the Phillies at the beginning of the season, was in the starting lineup. He came to bat with two outs in the third inning, and with the bases loaded belted the first pitch to him by Colorado Rockies hurler Aaron Cook into the right field bullpen. The blow led the Phillies to a 9-1 victory.

A first-hit slam hadn't happened in the National League in 35 years. Bobby Bonds did the honors in 1968. Of the two previous Phillies to perform the feat, one was hit by Bill Duggleby in 1898 and Jim Command drilled the other in 1954.

Duggleby, a pitcher, hit five other home runs in his career. Command, a third baseman, never homered again in 23 big league at-bats. As the 2006 season began, Utley had socked 43 home runs and was on his way to many more.

Names and Numbers

Naming stadiums after companies that pump lavish sums of money into a team's coffers has become one of the regular practices in professional sports. But some of the names are so ridiculous that one can only wonder when Viagra Field or Waste Removal Stadium will be making their debuts.

But that, of course, is one of the ways these days that a team produces revenue. Along with the gazillions taken in from super boxes, licensing, signage, and the ubiquitous TV networks, peddling the naming rights to a ballpark helps teams afford the bloated salaries that rule their complex balance sheets.

Many new stadiums are named after consumer goods. Hence, we have Minute Maid Park (do they serve orange juice instead of beer?), Petco Park (free gerbils are given away at each day game), and PNC Park (low-cost loans are available to anybody who buys a scorecard). And good old names such as Fenway Park, Wrigley Field, and Yankee Stadium are fading into the sunset.

If you think letting a company name a stadium in return for a big chunk of change is a relatively new idea, guess again. Back in 1970 when the politicians who ran Philadelphia were hunting for a name for the city's new multipurpose stadium, the city controller was a former basketball great named Tom Gola.

In a moment of heightened creativity, Gola made the brash suggestion that the city sell the naming rights to the new stadium that would be the home of the Phillies and Eagles. Doing that, Gola figured, might raise as much as $30 million in revenue.

Gola was practically laughed off the city council floor for making such a preposterous suggestion. Eventually, the venue, built at a cost of $52 million, was named Veterans Stadium.

Now, some 36 years later, the Phillies play in a $345-million palace called Citizens Bank Park. The ballpark is one of four sports venues located in the same area that houses the city's four major pro teams. Perhaps not so ironically—Philadelphia being a strong financial center—all four stadiums are named after banks.

Somewhere, Tom Gola has to be enjoying his special foresight.

Similar Seasons

Rare is the season that a baseball team captures the same number of wins two years in a row. Yet, it's happened three different times with the Phillies.

The team won 86 games in 2003. And it won 86 games in 2004. That matches the production of the 1907 and 1908 teams, each of which won 83 games, and the 1976 and 1977 clubs, which won 101 apiece.

The Phillies also won 86 games in 2001. That was the first of two times that a team managed by Larry Bowa won 86 games. (Bowa was not the manager for the team's final win in 2004.)

Four other Phillies managers have won the same number of games twice while piloting the Phillies. Bill Murray did it in 1907-1908 and Danny Ozark in both 1976 and 1977. Mayo Smith led the Phils to 77 wins in 1955 and 1957, while Gene Mauch was at the helm when the Phillies won 87 in 1963 and 1966.

Heading South

Each February, a truck leaves Philadelphia loaded with items that the Phillies will use at their spring training base in Clearwater,

Florida. And it's not filled with golf clubs, suntan lotion, beach chairs, and fishing poles.

Thousands of items that will be used on the baseball diamond are packed into a 48-foot-long, nine-foot-high, seven-foot-wide trailer-tractor. They'll be used by the more than 50 players and 20-plus other uniformed personnel who participate in the six-week preseason sessions.

What are some of these items? How about 12,000 baseballs? There are 1,200 caps. And 1,140 bats, 550 pairs of pants, 400 T-shirts, 250 warmup jackets, 150 jerseys, and 150 batting helmets.

The big rig also contains 10,000 pieces of gum. Two thousand coat hangers. There are 840 bars of soap, 800 towels, 100 equipment bags, and 50 rosin bags. Included in the load are 24 cases of sunflower seeds, 20 cases of powder, and 15 gallons of grass stain remover.

Of course, if somebody does want to stick in a set of golf clubs or a fishing pole—even if it's somebody from the media—that's okay, too.

Home Run Extravaganza

Used to be, the sole attraction at an All-Star Game was the All-Star Game. No frills. No sideshows. No carnivals. No special events. The chief focus was a game that had the best players in the land competing.

The simplicity of such an event, of course, has changed. Now, it's a two-day extravaganza that comes off as a bad imitation of the Mardi Gras. It's supposed to provide the fans with some extra entertainment although it's highly debatable whether that is really necessary.

One element of the circus is an event called the Home Run Derby. Some of the best hitters in captivity attempt to swat the feeble tosses of batting practice pitchers into the next county. Once in a great while, the event is even exciting.

Such was the case at the 2005 All-Star festivities at Detroit's Comerica Park when on the night before the actual game and with a crowd of 41,004 watching, Phillies right fielder Bobby Abreu gave new meaning to the definition of a long-distance clouter. Abreu not only won the Home Run Derby, he mashed balls with such Ruthian fervor that the winner's trophy should be renamed in his honor.

Overall, Abreu blasted 41 pitches for "home runs." On merit, the number is almost unfathomable, even if Abreu was merely hitting lobs tossed by Phillies bullpen coach Ramon Henderson. And it exceeded by a staggering 14 homers the previous high stroked in the 2004 contest by Miguel Tejada.

The format of the contest departed from its predecessors by having each of the eight combatants represent a different country. Thus, Abreu represented his native Venezuela. Mark Teixreira (United States), Jason Bay (Canada), Ivan Rodriguez (Puerto Rico), David Ortiz (Dominican Republic), Andruw Jones (Caraçao), Carlos Lee (Panama), and Hee-Seop Choi (South Korea) completed the lineup.

Abreu got off to a quick start in the first round, belting two of the first five pitches into the stands. A little later he rammed five straight tosses out of the park and eight of nine pitches outta there. One of them traveled 517 feet. Another hit the top of an umbrella sitting near a barbecue pit. By the time the round ended, Abreu had not only chipped his bat, but had smacked a single-round record 24 home runs, exceeding by nine the mark previously held by Tejada.

With the lineup reduced for the second round and the crowd chanting, "Bobby, Bobby, Bobby," Abreu added six more long clouts. Then, pitted against Rodriguez in the final round, he drilled 11 shots into the bleachers to win the contest with ease.

Even Abreu, who was offered a total of 157 pitches and took 71 swings (hitting 58 percent of them out), was surprised.

"I couldn't believe what I was doing," said the eight-year Phillies veteran. "I was so excited. It's amazing. I don't know if I'll be able to sleep."

Abreu who batted in the leadoff spot in the actual game, had up to that point hit 18 homers during the regular season. Did the

Bobby Abreu celebrates his Home Run Derby win during the 2005 All-Star Game. *Rich Pilling/Getty Images*

derby win foul up his swing? Following the festivities, Abreu went into a prolonged slump and hit just six home runs the rest of the season.

Errors in Excess

Over the years, the Phillies have not been immune to big innings. They scored 13 times in a single inning in a game in 2003, and they pushed across 12 in one inning in a skirmish in 1923. They even scored three runs in the 19th inning of a game in 1919.

It's unlikely, though, that any big inning was more bizarre than the ninth frame of a game late in the 2005 season against the Florida Marlins. The Phils scored 10 runs—a club record for the ninth inning—which was their entire production in a 10-2 victory at Pro Player Stadium.

It wasn't so much *that* the runs scored. It was *how* they scored. The Phillies got eight hits—all singles. But they took advantage of four errors and several other misplays by the Marlins, launching the rally after barely touching the offerings of premier pitcher Dontrelle Willis for eight innings.

"We played like the Bad News Bears out there," lamented manager Jack McKeon about his Marlins miscues.

The bad news began when Jimmy Rollins hit a bouncer that hopped on the hard turf over the head of third baseman Mike Lowell. Two batters later, Bobby Abreu drilled a hard grounder that second baseman Luis Castillo muffed for the first error, allowing the first Phillies run.

That sent Willis to the showers. Pat Burrell then hit a sky-high fly to shallow center that should've been caught but fell for a single. On the play, another run scored when center fielder Juan Pierre overran the ball. Then Chase Utley followed with a bunt single and went to second as pitcher Todd Jones threw the ball past first base, a third Phillies run coming home.

Next up, David Bell hit a catchable short fly that dropped between Castillo and Pierre for an RBI hit. Mike Lieberthal's single added a fifth run. It was followed by first baseman Jeff Conine's error on a grounder by Ryan Howard that let in another tally.

After Michael Tucker's hit, the Phillies scored two more runs on Rollins's single. With the Phils leading 8-2, the Marlins finally got their first out. Then Endy Chavez's single to center was booted by Pierre, and another run crossed. Shane Victorino followed with a sacrifice fly to drive in the final run of what was an ugly nightmare for the Marlins.

The Phillies, however, had no complaints.

"Sometimes, things happen in strange ways," said Phils manager Charlie Manuel in a marvelous understatement.

"The whole thing was strange," Burrell added.

And indeed, it was.

Hitting Streaks

During the first four years of Jimmy Rollins's big league career, it never would have occurred to anyone to mention him in the same sentence as Ed Delahanty.

After all, Delahanty was one of the Phillies' greatest players of all time, a Hall of Famer who hit over .400 three times and was holder of the fourth-highest batting average (.346) in big league history. Rollins had mostly been known as an ultra-swift baserunner, a sure-handed fielder, and a little guy (five feet, eight inches tall) who too often swung for the fences and who had a strong aversion to talking pitches although he was the Phils' primary leadoff hitter.

The relationship, however, changed in 2005 when Rollins threatened, then broke Delahanty's club record for hitting in the most consecutive games. Although he had previously never hit in more than 12 straight games, the Phillies shortstop ended the season with a 36-game hitting streak, along the way passing Delahanty's ancient 31-game mark set in 1899.

Following the game in which he broke the record, Rollins was asked what he knew about Delahanty.

"Somebody told me he went over Niagara Falls in a barrel," Rollins said. "That's all I know about him."

Rollins was given the wrong information. Although Delahanty did indeed go over the falls, he hardly had the protection of a barrel. As any student of Phillies history knows, Big Ed was either pushed, jumped, or fell into the Niagara River and was carried over the falls to his death in a tragic accident in 1903.

Actually, it was not known that Delahanty owned the Phillies' consecutive-game hitting streak until late in Rollins's run. For many years, Billy Hamilton was thought to hold the club record at 36.

But in checking the record, the Phillies learned that during his apparent streak, Hamilton had gone hitless in three trips to the plate in a game that was protested. It had been assumed that the protest had been upheld and that the game was thrown out, thereby allowing Sliding Billy's streak to continue.

Not so, said researchers. Hamilton's streak had actually stopped at 27. That was just one more game than Chuck Klein reached in 1930 when he had—not one but two—26-game streaks. These were sandwiched around a 14-game streak and ultimately resulted in Klein hitting safely in 70 of 73 games.

As for Rollins, who sparked a stretch drive that kept the Phillies in the wildcard race until the last day of the season, he finished the year with a career-high .290 batting average while reaching double figures in home runs, triples, doubles, and stolen bases for the fourth time in five seasons. His 36-game streak, accomplished by a seventh-inning single in the final game, was also the eighth-longest in big league history.

Rookie of the Year

On a day when a city transit strike, upcoming elections, and an absurdity named Terrell Owens dominated the pages and airwaves of the local media, the best sports story in Philadelphia in a long time was buried so deeply that many fans hardly knew it happened.

Jimmy Rollins (left) established a new club record with hits in 36 consecutive games. *Eliot J. Schechter/Getty Images*

There, beneath the fold of local papers and in a tag line on the early evening news, came the story of how a refreshing young power hitter was voted the National League's 2005 Rookie of the Year. Ryan Howard is his name.

A first baseman, the 25-year-old slugger easily outdistanced the rest of the field, landing 19 of the first-place votes cast by 32 baseball writers (two from each NL city). Adding his three second- and five third-place votes, Howard totaled 109 points, 31 more than runner-up Willy Taveras of the Houston Astros, who snared seven first-place votes.

Howard was just the fourth Phillies player to win the writers' award, joining Jack Sanford (1957), Dick Allen (1964), and Scott Rolen (1997). Del Ennis (1946), Richie Ashburn (1948), Ed

Bouchee (1957), Lonnie Smith (1980), and Juan Samuel (1984) were named top rookies by *The Sporting News*, but curiously those selections in recent years have been overshadowed by choices of the scribes.

An amiable fellow with a ready smile, Howard refused to allow himself to be swallowed up by the significance of the award.

"I just tried to do my best," he said. "It was just a matter of going out and playing hard every day."

Playing every day didn't begin for Howard until July 1 when he was recalled from the minors and replaced the injured Jim Thome. From then on, he played in 88 games, hitting 22 home runs—two of them game-winning grand slams—driving in 63 and batting .288 with a .567 slugging percentage. He cracked 11 homers and collected 27 RBI in the final month of the season.

Manager Charlie Manuel cited Howard's "passion for the game" and "his determination" while claiming that the two-time minor league MVP "loves to hit" and "the ball just jumps off his bat."

Batting coach Milt Thompson said, "Ryan's work ethic and his aggressiveness help to make him a good hitter."

When the award was announced in early November, Howard may have been the only Rookie of the Year ever named who was not assured of a starting position the following season. At the time, Thome's expected return meant that the Phillies had two outstanding players at the same position, and no easy way to solve the problem.

The problem, however, was eventually solved when the Phils traded Thome to the Chicago White Sox.

Howard was the third NL player to capture the rookie award while playing in fewer than 100 games. The others were Bob Horner (1978) and Willie McCovey (1959). One other Howard has earned the honor—Frank in 1960.

Chapter 11

The Best Era in Phillies History

2005-2011

The Straight Scoop

I n the long and occasionally memorable history of Phillies baseball, there has never been an era quite like the present one. It has truly been the Golden Era of the team that has been playing in Philadelphia for 129 years.

Two straight trips to the World Series and one World Championship, two National League pennants, and five straight postseason appearances, all preceded by three second place finishes. Starting in 2004 and continuing through 2011, the Phillies have done what no other Phillies team ever did before.

It all goes to show what making the right moves can do for a team. Build a farm system that produces key players Ryan Howard, Chase Utley, Jimmy Rollins, Carlos Ruiz, Cole Hamels, Vance Worley, and Ryan Madson, plus a host of players used in trades. Make major acquisitions by signing free agents or +trading for key position players such as Shane Victorino, Jayson Werth, Placido Polanco, Raul Ibanez, Hunter Pence, and pitchers such as Roy Halladay, Brad Lidge, Cliff Lee, Roy Oswalt, and Jamie Moyer.

170

Hire a manager named Charlie Manuel whose special brand of leadership produces glittering results. And erect a marvelous stadium that ranks among the best there is.

To all that can be added one more element. Give the fans a winner, and they will come. At Citizens Bank Park, that's just what the Phillies have done. More than three million fans in five straight years. Sellout crowds that by the end of the 2011 regular season numbered 204 in a row. A fan base of ultra-avid rooters who have easily made this Phillies team the most popular in Philadelphia sports history.

There once was a time when the Golden Era of Phillies baseball was considered to be the period that ran from 1975 through 1983. During those nine seasons, the Phils won their first World Series in 1980 and reached another Fall Classic in 1983. They won three straight East Division titles and five overall. But the Phillies of that era had an overall regular season record of 791-612 (.564) and a post-season mark of 15-21. In eight seasons, the current Phils are 732-564 (.565) from 2004 through 2011 during the regular season and 27-19 in the postseason.

Much of the current Phillies' success has been made possible by an astute managerial team led by president and CEO David Montgomery. Three general managers have contributed, starting with Ed Wade, who laid the groundwork for future Phillies teams, Pat Gillick, who on his way to a place in the Hall of Fame, kept the ball rolling with many masterful moves, and Ruben Amaro, Jr., who solidified the club's extraordinary success with the kinds of roster additions that most teams could only dream about.

Prior to the 2004 season, the Phillies had stumbled through a siege of mediocrity that since the club's 1993 trip to the World Series had produced nothing better than two second place finishes. But the dawdling franchise began to turn around in the fourth year of the 21st century when it ended its 33-year residency at Veterans Stadium and moved into the sparkling, new Citizens Bank Park.

Attracting more than three million fans for only the second time in team history (1993 was the first time) in 2004, the Phillies in Larry Bowa's fourth and final season as manager surged to a second place finish led by the hitting of Jim Thome and Bobby Abreu and the pitching of Brett Myers. Although Bowa was dismissed near the end of the season and replaced the following campaign by Manuel, the club's ascent had begun.

Under Manuel the Phils won 88 games in 2005, the club's highest victory total since 1993, and finished second again. Another second place finish followed in 2006 with the Phils just missing a wild-card spot by three wins. For the Phillies, though, happy days were here again, even though during the 2007 season the Phils became the first sports team ever to lose 10,000 games (a slightly erroneous description because the Washington Generals, patsy of the Harlem Globetrotters, have lost more than 16,000 games).

A new group had taken over top billing on the field. Howard, Utley, and Rollins were the team's stars now. And with that group leading the way, the Phils won the NL East Division title, coming from seven games behind in late August to finish first as the New York Mets lost 12 of their last 17 games, while the Phillies won 23 of their final 34 tests, including four of their last five games to win on the last day of the season. Unfortunately, in a follow-up to the Mets staging one of baseball's greatest collapses, the Phillies lost in three games to the Colorado Rockies in the NLDS.

Then, with Rollins insisting that "We're the team to beat," it was back again to the postseason in 2008. Only this time the results were perfect. After winning another division crown by finishing with a 13-3 record and coming from three and one-half games behind the Mets in mid-September, the Phillies roared through the playoffs, beating the Milwaukee Brewers in four games in the NLDS and the Los Angeles Dodgers in five games in the NLCS.

Then it was on to the World Series. In just their sixth trip to the Fall Classic, the Phillies won the second World Series in club history, beating the Tampa Bay Rays, four games to one. It was a scintillating Series, climaxed by a clinching victory that took two days to complete after rain had forced suspension of the game after five and one-half innings of play. Because of more rain the next day, play didn't resume until the second night after the first suspended game in World Series history. Pedro Feliz ripped a seventh inning single that scored Eric Bruntlett and gave the Phils a 4-3 victory. J. C. Romero won his second game of the Series in relief and Lidge got his second save in five games, climaxing a season in which he saved 41 games in 41 chances during the regular season and seven out of seven in the postseason. Two days after the end of the season, an estimated two-million fans jammed the center-city area as the Phillies paraded down Broad Street. Later, the Phillies were invited to Washington D.C. where they met President Obama in a festive affair at the White House.

With Hamels having emerged as one of the league's top pitchers and Lee arriving in Philadelphia in a stunning mid-season trade pulled off by Amaro, the Phillies returned to the World Series in 2009. To get there, the Phils won their division by six games over the Florida Marlins, capturing 93 wins during the regular season and winning their second straight pennant by downing the Rockies in four games in the NLDS and the Dodgers in five games in the NLCS. Against the New York Yankees in the Series, however, the Phillies fell in six games despite two wins by Lee and a record-tying two two-home run games by Utley.

But the Phillies' run was far from over. With another electrifying and wildly popular group of players that included Victorino, Werth, and Ibanez, and was bolstered first by the acquisition of Halladay and then by the mid-season trade for Oswalt, the 2010 Phils won their fourth straight division title. After roosting in second or third place from the end of May until early September, they moved into first place and posted a 97-65 record, the best in the big leagues and the team's highest win total since 1993. Halladay, who had pitched a perfect game during the season and with 21 victories had become the first Phillies first 20-game winner since Steve Carlton won 23 in 1982, hurled only the second no-hitter in post-season history when he beat the Cincinnati Reds in the first game of the NLDS. Subsequently, the Phils swept the Reds in three games, but then lost to the San Francisco Giants in six games in the NLCS.

That was just one of two devastating losses for the Phillies. During the season, much-loved broadcaster Harry Kalas passed away in the booth as he prepared to go on the air for a Phillies game in Washington. The golden-voiced Kalas had been a Phils broadcaster since 1971.

It was back to the top in 2011. With a pitching staff that was being called The Four Aces (Halladay, Lee, Hamels, and Oswalt) and a robust offense, the Phillies quickly established themselves as the team to beat. After leading the East Division for all but one day in the first half and for the entire second half, the Phillies became the fastest team to capture 90 victories in club history when they reached that mark in early September. They claimed their 97th in mid-September, moving a staggering club record-tying 46 games over .500.

With the best record in the big leagues for the second straight year, the Phillies clinched no worse than a wild card spot in the playoffs in their 146th game, the earliest that ever happed to a Phils team. It was the first time any team in Philadelphia sports history (including the Athletics) reached postseason play five times in a row. Four games later, they won the East Division with their 98th win, again the earliest clinching date in Phils history.

Eight straight losses, however, followed the clincher and temporarily blurred the Phillies' vast accomplishments. But the club ended with three straight victories to finish the season with a club-record 102th win on the last day of the season, surpassing the old mark of 101 set by both the 1976 and 1977 teams. The joyride, however, ended quickly one week later when the Phillies bowed in five games of the NLDS to the St. Louis Cardinals, tossing away a two games to one lead and collapsing in the final game with a 1-0 defeat.

Awards Aplenty

There has been no lack of awards for members of recent Phillies teams. Special honors have been numerous, making the period from 2004 to the present one of the most individually decorated eras in club history.

Among the top honors in baseball, Ryan Howard in 2006 and Jimmy Rollins in 2007 both won National League Most Valuable Player Awards. Of their seven MVPs in history, the Phillies haven't hadn't had one since Mike Schmidt won his third in 1986.

Howard was also NL Rookie of the Year in 2005. One year later, he became only the second player in major league history (Cal Ripken, Jr., was the first) to win back-to-back Rookie of the Year and MVP awards.

Roy Halladay won the NL's Cy Young Award in 2010, the second of his career, and the seventh in club history. The last one was captured by Steve Bedrosian in 1987. In 2010, Halladay was also named Major League Player of the Year by *Baseball America* and Pro Athlete of the Year by *The Sporting News*. In 2011, three Phils pitchers ranked in the top five in the Cy Young voting, the first time that's ever happened in Philadelphia. Halladay placed second, Cliff Lee was third, and Cole Hamels placed fifth.

Brad Lidge was voted NL honors as NL Rolaids Relief Man in 2008. Phillies players also sopped up post-season honors with Cole Hamels in 2008 and Howard in 2009 collecting NL Championship Series MVP awards. Hamels was also named MVP of the 2008 World Series.

In recent years, Phillies players have earned nine Gold Glove Awards, including three each by Shane Victorino (2008, 2009, 2010) and Rollins (2007, 2008, 2009). Bobby Abreu (2005), Aaron Rowand (2007), and Placido Polanco (2011) claimed the others.

Since 2004, 16 different Phillies players have been voted to represent the National League in the All-Star Game. Chase Utley leads the pack with five selections, followed by Howard with three. Others named include Halladay, Hamels, Victorino, and Abreu with two apiece, and Rollins, Lidge, Jim Thome, Billy Wagner, Tom Gordon, Rowand, Raul Ibanez, Jayson Werth, Cliff Lee, and

Placido Polando, each one time. In 2011, the Phillies had three pitchers—Halladay, Lee, and Hamels—named to the All-Star team for the first time in club history. That year, all but one member (Carlos Ruiz) of the club's starting lineup had been on an All-Star team.

•

Manuel Moves to the Top

In a magnificent season, Charlie Manuel passed The Wizard of Oz, The Father of Professional Baseball, and finally The Little General to become the winningest Phillies manager of all time.

With a victory in the final game of the season, Manuel finished 2011 with 646 wins, along the way moving ahead of Danny Ozark (594), Harry Wright (636), and Gene Mauch (645).

It has taken Manuel just seven seasons to reach his current total, whereas Wright needed ten years and Mauch nine years. Neither of them ever finished in first place and each had some losing seasons.

While finishing the 2011 season as the oldest manager in Phillies history, the 67-year-old Manuel is the only Phils skipper to lead his team to two World Series and five East Division titles. While also finishing second twice, the one-time pilot of the Cleveland Indians (2000-2002) has never had a losing record with the Phillies, and his 102 victories in 2011 set a record as the highest total of wins in Phillies history (Ozark, led the 1976 and 1977 clubs to 101 regular season wins during his seven-year tenure.).

In 2009, Manuel became the first Phillies pilot to win 85 or more games five years in a row. Following the 2011 campaign, he had also led the Phils to four straight seasons of 92 or more wins. His 646-488 record gives him a winning percentage of .570, the second highest mark of all Phillies managers, ranking just behind Arthur Irwin (.575), and ahead of Steve O'Neil and Dallas Green (each .565).

Despite such records, the modest manager shuns personal credit. "The players are the ones who win games," he said. "When we win a championship or I reach a milestone or get an award, it's because they made it possible."

A No-Hitter for the Books

The no-hitter pitched by Roy Halladay in the first game of the 2010 National League Division Series was a remarkable feat that should be viewed as one of the greatest achievements in Phillies history.

A good case can also be made that it was one of the greatest games ever pitched in the major leagues.

No pitching performance, of course, matches the perfect game hurled by the New York Yankees' Don Larsen in the fifth game of the 1956 World Series. Larsen's 2-0 victory over the Brooklyn Dodgers before an incredulous crowd of 64,519 at Yankee Stadium was a magnificent achievement of unfathomable proportions.

But so was Halladay's. With his 4-0 victory over the Cincinnati Reds in a game in which he struck out eight and allowed only one batter to reach base, Halladay joined Larsen as the only pitchers ever to hurl a no-hitter in post-season play.

Given the significance of the game, the surroundings, the pitcher's own history, and the fact that he allowed no hits in a most crucial battle, Halladay takes a back seat to no one except Larsen when it comes to rating baseball's greatest pitching performances.

Like Larsen's blanking the defending World Champion Dodgers with a lineup featuring four future Hall of Famers, Halladay's no-hitter was especially noteworthy because he was pitching against the team with the best offense in the National League.

While winning the Central Division title, Cincinnati led the league in batting average, runs, hits, total bases, home runs, RBI, and slugging percentage. Led by first baseman Joey Votto, who later became the league's Most Valuable Player, the Reds fielded a lineup that included four players with 20 or more home runs and four starters hitting above .280.

There were 46,411 people—at the time, the third largest crowd in the history of Citizens Bank Park—in the stands. Excitement spread across the stadium like a monumental blanket. Rally towels and red clothing clogged the seats. The noise was deafening.

Halladay had the added pressure of pitching for the first time in post-season play. In nine full seasons and parts of three others with the Toronto Blue Jays, he had never appeared in the playoffs. And although he said later that he was more "excited than nervous," the heavy demands of such a situation could hardly be ignored.

Since the mound was moved back to 60- feet, six- inches from home plate in 1893, there have been 238 no-hitters, including 18 perfect games, counting Halladay's in May against the Florida Marlins.

That game, incidentally, made the Phillies the only team in National League history that has had two pitchers throw perfect games. Nearly one-half century earlier, Jim Bunning fired a perfecto for the Phils in 1964.

Who'd Have Believed It?

Nobody ever labeled the Phillies as practitioners of the status quo. This is a team that from its very beginning has specialized in being unusual.

In recent years, that definition has continued to be evident. The Phillies had an author among their midst. Catcher Chris Coste penned a highly interesting autobiography called The 33-Year-Old Rookie. Left fielder Pat Burrell often brought his dog, a Mastiff named Elvis, into the clubhouse. Pitcher Jamie Moyer was still pitching at the age of 47 and still reaching milestones, one of which occurred in 2008 when he became the second oldest pitcher (Phil Niekro was the first in 1985) to win 16 games in one season. And Jayson Werth's grandfather (Ducky Schofield), uncle (Dick Schofield), and stepfather (Dennis Werth) all played in the big leagues.

In 2009 against the New York Mets, reserve second baseman Eric Bruntlett made the second unassisted triple play in Phillies history (Mickey Morandini's was the first) and only the second tri-play in baseball history that ended a game. Joe Blanton became the first Phillies pitcher ever to hit a home run in the World Series when he socked a four-bagger in a 2008 game against the Tampa Bay Rays that he won. Carlos Ruiz stole home in a 2007 game, the first time a Phillies catcher had done that in 25 years (the last was Bo Diaz).

Ryan Howard made an appearance on the earthy but highly popular television show called Entourage. Infielder Wilson Valdez made an appearance on the pitching mound for the first time in his pro career, and in one inning of work got the win. Shane Victorino got ejected while arguing balls and strikes from center field. And Vance Worley not only won more games in a row (nine) than any Phils rookie before him, but was also the first player of Chinese descent to perform in a Phillies uniform.

In 1981, the Phillies made one of their worst trades in history by sending minor league infielder Ryne Sandberg and shortstop Larry Bowa to the Chicago Cubs for highly mediocre shortstop Ivan DeJesus. Sandberg, went on to a career that led him into the Hall of Fame while the Phillies endured years of persecution for such a horrendous mistake. Don't you know, nearly 30 years later, Sandberg finally came back to the Phils when they hired him to manage their Triple-A farm team, the Lehigh Valley Iron Pigs. In his first season in 2011, Sandberg led the Pigs to the International League Governor's Cup championship series before losing to the Columbus Clippers.

The Magic Date

When the Phillies' success in the early part of the 21st century is fully analyzed, it might be a good idea for the city of Philadelphia to consider declaring July 29 as a holiday. That's a date that figures heavily in the club's accomplishments.

On July 29, 2009, the club acquired pitcher Cliff Lee and outfielder Ben Francisco in a six-player trade with the Cleveland Indians. Lee went on to win seven of 11 decisions during the regular season and four out of four in the post-season, including two in the World Series.

One year later on July 29, the Phillies sent three players to the Houston Astros for pitcher Roy Oswalt. Oswalt then posted a 7-1 record, plus another win in the NLCS as the Phils went to the last round of the National League playoffs.

On July 29, 2011, the Phillies once again made a major move when they swapped four minor league prospects to the Astros for outfielder Hunter Pence. When he came to the Phils, Pence said "It was like joining an All-Star team." Subsequently, he helped the Phillies to their fifth straight division title.

Ironically, the general manager at Houston when the last two deals were made was ex-Phillies GM Ed Wade. Originally an assistant GM with the Phillies, Wade assumed the head job in 1997 and held it through 2004. After taking over as the Astros' GM in 2007, Wade was also responsible for trading reliever Brad Lidge to the Phillies.

In recent years, the Phillies have been led by two general managers who made blockbuster deals that wound up solidifying the team's spot as the most successful major league franchise during the period from 2004 through 2011.

Wade's successor, 2011 Hall of Fame inductee Pat Gillick, made trades that brought Lidge, Joe Blanton, and Jamie Moyer to the Phillies. He also signed valuable free agents, including Jayson Werth, Greg Dobbs, Pedro Feliz, and J.C. Romero.

When he took over after Gillick retired at the end of the 2008 season, Ruben Amaro, Jr., began a career that would make him one of the most—if not the most—successful wheeler-dealers in Phillies history. Amaro's deals landed a raft full of superstars, not the least of whom were Lee, Oswalt, and Pence.

Amaro had traded away Lee, but got him back, signing him as a free agent at the end of 2010. He also signed free agents Raul Ibanez, Placido Polanco (who had been traded away by Gillick in 2005), Pedro Martinez, and Brian Schneider, all of whom played key roles in the club's success.

Of his many blockbuster deals, however, none made by Amaro

was any greater than the one in late 2009 when he sent three prospects to the Toronto Blue Jays for pitcher Roy Halladay. With a no-hitter and a perfect game, 21 wins, and ultimately the National League Cy Young Award, Halladay had one of the greatest seasons of any pitcher in Phillies history. In 2011, he followed that up with 19-6 record, thus becoming the first Phils hurler to win 40 games in two consecutive seasons since Steve Carlton did it in 1979-80.

The Best Fans in Philly

When Hunter Pence was acquired by the Phillies in a mid-season deal in 2011, Phillies fans reacted predictably. They went crazy.

The Phillies had a night game shortly after the trade was made. The Phils' win over the Pittsburgh Pirates was followed by a fireworks display, Afterward, team officials decided to show a video on the big scoreboard at Citizens Bank Park of general manager Ruben Amaro, Jr., announcing the deal to the media a few hours earlier.

Public address announcer Dan Baker made the introduction. Then Amaro came on the screen. "I would like to announce that the Phillies have acquired outfielder Hunter Pence in a trade with the Houston Astros," Amaro began. Fans starting to leave the ballpark stopped in their tracks. The whole ballpark erupted in wild cheers.

When Pence arrived the following night, fans responded as would be expected. They gave him a standing ovation when he first appeared on the field during batting practice, again when Baker announced the starting lineups, a third time when he took the field in the first inning, and finally one more time when he came to bat for the first time.

The celebration amply demonstrated the uncontested adulation Phillies fans show for their team. With sellout crowds of 44,000 or more every night and more than three million in attendance each of the last five seasons, Phillies fans have moved to the top of the list among followers of Philadelphia sports teams. No other team even comes close.

In mid-season in 2011, the Phillies drew the 25 millionth fan to watch a game at CBP. The feat was accomplished in less than eight seasons. It took 12 years to reach that number at Veterans Stadium.

Since moving to CBP in 2004, the Phillies have draw more than three million fans in six different seasons altogether, including a record 3,680,718 in 2011, the first time the team has ever led the major leagues in attendance for the season. Some 1,153,761 fans have watched 25 post-season games at CBP, including a record 46,575 in Game Two of the 2011 NLDS. Since they moved in, the Phils have sold out CBP 380 times in 648 regular-season games, and have sold out the 43,651-seat stadium 204 times in a row by the end of the 2011 campaign.

"It definitely motivates you once you get them going," Jimmy Rollins said of Phillies fans raucous support of the team. At all games, a sea of red splashes across the stadium as most fans come dressed in some part of clothing that shows the Phillies' primary color.

The Phillies averaged 2,083,000 fans per season over a 33-year period at the Vet. By contrast, the team has averaged 3,250,000 fans per season at CBP. With such avid followers, is it any wonder the fans welcomed Pence to Philadelphia they way that they did?

It's like Cliff Lee said when he returned to Philadelphia before the 2011 season. Asked why he wanted to come back to Philly when he could've signed for more money with the New York Yankees, Lee said, when it comes to sports, "This is the place to be."

Chapter 12

The Last Word

Views from the Press Box

The Straight Scoop

Hard as it might be for some people to believe, Pulitzer Prize-winning columnist Red Smith worked in Philadelphia during his early days in the newspaper business. Smith covered the Phillies for the now-defunct *Philadelphia Record.*

As was the case then and continued to be throughout his career, Smith wrote colorfully and with special insight. And reporting about the Phillies playing at Baker Bowl gave him considerable opportunity to hone the skills that would lead to his becoming a renowned columnist with *The New York Times.*

During Smith's days in Philadelphia, Baker Bowl, a shabby relic that was falling apart in every conceivable way, was on its deathbed. That condition didn't escape Smith. He called it "a cobwebby House of Horrors." Later he described the park more graphically.

"It bore a striking resemblance to a rundown men's room," he wrote.

It's a Girl

Phillies games were first broadcast in 1936 when the club played at Baker Bowl. Unlike the slick broadcasting facilities of today, a front-row seat in the lower deck served as the spot from which the broadcasters would make their pronouncements.

Before he became an anchorman on network television in New York, Taylor Grant was one of the early Phillies broadcasters. Often, when Phils players warmed up before games, Grant would join in, playing pepper and tossing the old pill around while dressed in coat and tie.

Grant was at his post in the stands one day when an usher raced up to him, right in the middle of a game. "You just had a daughter," the usher yelled. Of course, the mike was open. And that is how baseball listeners throughout the area learned that the man behind the mike had just become a father.

Yo, Bill

In the days before pregame, postgame, and during-the-game shows became the norm in baseball, Philadelphia television had a little break in the action called *Grandstand Manager*. The host was Bill Duncan, an old-time sportswriter turned broadcaster. Duncan pontificated between games of doubleheaders at Shibe Park from a small section of the upper deck that jutted out from the regular grandstand.

Along with Duncan's comments, the show usually included an interview with a player. Once, Phillies outfielder Bill Nicholson was being interviewed. Showing no particular inclination for diplomacy, Duncan came right out with it.

"Bill," he said, "you used to be a good ballplayer. What happened to you?"

Unofficial Scorer

Gene Kelly became the Phillies' play-by-play man in 1950. With his rapid style of delivery and sense of humor, the six-foot, seven-inch broadcaster quickly developed a following.

Kelly became noted as the broadcaster who coined the phrase "Ballantine Blast," using a sponsor's name when calling a home run by a Phillies hitter. Another Kellyism was "Whiteflash [after an Atlantic product] Whifferoo," used to describe a strikeout. (Were these one of the first times a sports announcer shamelessly worked a sponsor's name into his broadcasts?)

One night, the Phillies were playing a game in Los Angeles. The clash had started at 11 p.m. Eastern Time, and it was still in progress at 1:30 a.m. After one particular play, Kelly tried to be helpful.

"For those of you scoring in bed," he said, "that play went ..."

Mayo Who?

When Mayo Smith was named the Phillies' manager in 1955, he arrived as an obscure career minor leaguer whose only taste of big league life—such as it was—came in a brief fling with the 1945 Philadelphia Athletics. Smith had no previous experience as a major league manager, qualifying him as the proverbial unknown.

A press conference was called to introduce the new skipper. The assembled scribes waited anxiously to learn his identity. Finally, the moment arrived. Mayo Smith, it was proclaimed, is the new manager of the Phillies.

And almost as if it had been rehearsed, the entire press corps shouted in unison, "Who?" No one knew who he was. Even outgoing manager Terry Moore said, "I never heard of the man."

Take Your Pick

In the days before designated hitters, six-inning pitchers, and artificial turf became disturbingly affiliated with baseball, sportswriters were often known to have a drink or two. They did even before or while they were covering games.

A writer for *The Philadelphia Inquirer* who shall be anonymous was supposed to be covering the Phillies in the game in which New York Giants pitcher Sal Maglie threw a no-hitter. Trouble was, he was too drunk to record the feat. So, as good Samaritans, five other writers covering the game filed stories for the guy. None of the writers knew each of the others was doing it. When the articles reached *The Inquirer*, the sports editor was delighted with his good fortune. He could, after all, use the best piece written.

What Did He Say?

One of the most recognizable names in Philadelphia broadcasting is surely By Saam. The colorful Texan called baseball games in Philadelphia from 1938 to 1975, which meant he handled play-by-play for a longer period than anybody else in the city. By his calculation, that amounted to more than 8,000 games.

Given the fact that he broadcast games of the mostly downtrodden Athletics and the often woebegone Phillies, Saam figured that he sat in the booth for more losing games than anybody in the history of the world. That claim notwithstanding, Saam was the first local broadcaster to be honored in the broadcasters' wing of the Baseball Hall of Fame in 1990.

Although unintentional, one of Saam's distinguishing characteristics was his occasional linguistic slippage. Once, when coming on the air, he made a priceless switch.

"Hi, By Saam," he said, "this is everybody."

Another time in spring training, Saam was discussing the snowmobile accident involving Rennie Stennett of the Pittsburgh Pirates. By said he wasn't sure "if it happened down here or up north."

Saam often said, "Right you are," to show agreement with a point being made by a fellow boothmate. While broadcasting a World Series with Mel Allen, the veteran New York announcer gave By a nice introduction.

Said Allen, "I'm going to turn the broadcast over now to one of the most knowledgeable sportscasters, a man with a great voice, and a brilliant broadcaster."

To which Saam replied, "Right you are, Mel."

In a hotel lobby once, someone pointed out a woman seated nearby.

"See her," the guy said to Saam. "A mortal lock." Passing the woman a few minutes later, the amiable Saam gave her a friendly greeting.

"How are you doing, Mortal?" he asked. "Do you know Don Lock on our ballclub?"

On Deadline

In its declining years, Connie Mack Stadium was surrounded by a somewhat less than genteel neighborhood. Undesirables cluttered the area, and muggings and other unpleasantries occurred all too frequently.

The media, leaving as it did long after the park had cleared out, was particularly vulnerable. A splendid example of this took place one night when sportswriter Harry Hoffman, a scribe with the *Atlantic City Press*, was attempting to call in his story from the downstairs concourse.

As he dictated his story to the deskman at the other end of the phone, a would-be robber approached Hoffman and stuck a knife to his throat.

"Hold on a minute," Hoffman said to the deskman, "I've got a guy with a knife at my throat."

And the deskman replied, "Tell him you're on deadline."

At that point, the robber panicked and ran away.

Their Own Worst Enemy

For more than 30 years, Bill Conlin has been an astute observer of the game of baseball. And as a writer with the *Philadelphia Daily News*, he can turn a phrase with the best of them.

Covering the Phillies has allowed Conlin to exercise his considerable expertise through the written word in ways that range from caustic to humorous. Of his many great lines down through the years, one of his best was penned in 1977 after the Phillies had lost the third game of the league championship series with the Los Angeles Dodgers. (The series would end the next night when Tommy John beat the Phils in the rain.)

The Phillies had a 5-3 lead entering the ninth inning. But a series of miscues vetoed a probable win for the Phils. The worst of them was Greg Luzinski's inability to hold a deep fly by pinch-hitter Manny Mota on a ball that would've been easily caught if defensive specialist Jerry Martin had been in the game, as he should have been. That, and some other inopportune plays by the Phillies, including an error by second baseman Ted Sizemore, led to a 6-5 Dodgers victory.

At the end of his story that night, Conlin wrote, "The Phillies had met the enemy, and it was them."

Switching Stories

Sportswriters are always in search of good stories. Such was the case one day when Ralph Bernstein of The Associated Press found the Phillies' great slugger Dick Allen switch-hitting during batting practice.

Bernstein asked Allen if he was serious.

"Oh yeah," said Allen, who then delivered a lengthy lecture on the value of being a switch-hitter.

Bernstein took copious notes, then ascended to the press box to write his story.

As he was pounding away on something called a typewriter, creating prose that described how one of the game's top hitters was experimenting with switch-hitting, Bernstein was approached by Ray Kelly, the veteran baseball writer with the *Evening Bulletin*.

"What are you writing?" asked Kelly, who had been typing out his own piece.

When Bernstein told him, Kelly threw up his hands and burst out laughing. Pulling the paper out of his typewriter, Kelly showed Bernstein the article he was writing. It said that Allen was just kidding about becoming a switch-hitter.

A little later, not too happy with the turn of events, Bernstein cornered Allen in the Phillies clubhouse.

"Why did you give us opposite stories?" he demanded to know.

"You guys like different stories, don't you?" a chuckling Allen replied.

Fightin' Words

The 1960s and 1970s were a particularly contentious time in the relations of the media and Phillies players. It was particularly fashionable for the members of the print press to critique the team's performance with a heavy caustic touch and in ways that emphasized the snide and the sarcastic.

Naturally, members of the Phillies cast rebelled. Once, Danny Ozark took a poke at a writer, missing him only because clubhouse manager Kenny Bush deflected the shot. John Denny tried to punch one writer, thinking he was another scribe.

Some players—particularly Steve Carlton and Ron Reed—wouldn't talk to the media. Others hid in off-limits areas when the press came into the clubhouse. And still others gave monosyllabic answers.

Mike Schmidt provided his view of the adversarial relationship.

"Philadelphia," he said, "is the only city where you can experience the thrill of victory and the agony of reading about it the next morning."

Special Delivery

The stories about the broadcasting career of Richie Ashburn are legendary. The man who coined the phrase, "Hard to believe, Harry," had a dry, Midwestern wit that often led to some of local broadcasting's funniest lines.

There was the time, for instance, when the Phillies decided to ban all on-air references to purveyors of food except sponsors. At the time, food was regularly being delivered to the broadcast booth, both by fans and by commercial establishments. The servers were saluted on the air. One of Ashburn's favorite dishes was the pizza often sent to the booth by the Calebrese twin brothers, who were not among the ranks of Phillies advertisers.

Phillies broadcasters always announced birthday greetings to fans over the air. But with the food ban in effect, it was a different story. One night, though, craving some of the brothers' tasty pizza, Ashburn decided to take matters into his own hands.

"I want to send out a special birthday greeting to the Calebrese twins, Plain and Pepperoni," he announced.

Fifteen minutes later, two pizzas showed up at the booth.

◆ ◆ ◆

Ashburn and Harry Kalas did their first game together in 1971. The two would cherish their partnership for the next 26 years.

During that first year, Ashburn and Kalas were doing a spring training game when a player broke his bat. A discussion ensued about what players did to take care of their bats.

"When I was on a hot streak, I was always afraid to leave my bat in the clubhouse," Ashburn volunteered. "If I was on the road, I often took the bat back to the hotel and took it to bed with me."

Kalas expressed surprise at such an unusual practice.

"Actually," said Ashburn, "I've slept with a lot of old bats."

◆ ◆ ◆

Once, after Ashburn had done a pregame show, he returned to the booth only to be told that the interview he had just conducted was not picked up by the tape recorder.

"There's nothing on the tape," a technician said.

Later, Ashburn described the session as "the greatest interview I ever did."

Ashburn scurried back to the field, and as game time drew near, he redid the interview. After the game, he was waiting for the team bus to go back to the hotel when he was approached by a hooker.

"I'll do anything for $100," she said.

"How about the pregame show?" Ashburn responded.

It's Outta Here

It wouldn't take many fingers to count baseball's greatest broadcasters. You could comfortably do it on two hands. Harry Kalas, of course, would make the first hand.

Kalas has broadcast Phillies games from 1971 to the present. Over that time, he has become an icon in the Philadelphia area, his resonant voice being a familiar—and pleasing—sound to baseball fans throughout the region. Kalas was justly rewarded for his exceptional broadcasting career when he was named the 2002 winner of the Ford Frick Award and was honored in the broadcasters' wing of the Baseball Hall of Fame.

Every noted broadcaster has some signature calls, and Harry has his. "There's a long drive…it's outta here," Kalas intones. If it happened to be hit by the Phillies Hall of Fame third baseman, he would add to his call, "Home run by Michael Jack Schmidt."

Battle of the Sexes

When women began entering clubhouses in pursuit of their jobs as sportswriters, players showed their displeasure in a variety of ways. Some went to the off-limits areas, some ignored the women as though they weren't there, and some even became downright vulgar in a vain attempt to chase away the intruders.

In the Phillies' clubhouse, curtains were often hung over players' lockers. One particular relief pitcher had his own way of dealing with the situation. He would drop small but lit firecrackers at the women's feet. Other players finally had to tell him to cease and desist.

Trading Places

One year in spring training, the Phillies were scheduled to travel to Puerto Rico to play an exhibition game in honor of the late Roberto Clemente. Most of the players were willing to make the trip, but one of them, left fielder Greg Luzinski wasn't.

When the Phils slugger was told he had to go, he was sufficiently annoyed that he came into the clubhouse and decided to see how well he could swing a bat indoors. He homered off Steve Carlton's locker, a radio, and several other items that couldn't pitch.

Ralph Bernstein, the veteran Associated Press sportswriter, verified the incident, then wrote about it. The night of the day that the article appeared in print, Bernstein went to a familiar restaurant on Clearwater Beach. Luzinski was there, too. "The Bull" grabbed the writer and demanded to know why he'd written the story.

Bernstein replied, "If you don't tell me how to write, I won't tell you how to hit."

A Dead Run

Of the 240 inside-the-park home runs hit by the Phillies since 1900, probably none was hit by a slower runner than catcher Bob Boone. The Stanford graduate could think, and, of course, he could catch and hit, but when it came to running the bases, Boone might have had trouble beating a three-legged cow.

Some years after Boone's 1980 journey around the bases, a writer was digesting the Phils' list of inside-the-parkers when he came across the future big league manager's name. Curious about how such an improbable play could occur, the writer sought clarification from Phillies public relations director Larry Shenk.

"There must have been something freaky about that play," the writer suggested.

"Yeah, there was," responded Shenk with a straight face. "Three outfielders died."

Your Attention, Please

Ever wonder if players pay attention to the introductions they receive each time they come to bat? Guess what? They do.

Dan Baker has been the Phillies' popular public address announcer for some 34 years, and he has encountered virtually every situation. And that includes both sides of the coin.

Baker's pronouncements have usually been saluted, but once in a while they've been chastised. Various players, including in recent years the Phillies' Bobby Abreu and Jimmy Rollins, have looked up at Baker in his press box booth and signaled their approval of Dan's introduction. Conversely, he's been accused—although unjustifiably—of making derisive intros of visiting players, particularly J.D. Drew, the outfielder who shunned the Phillies after they made him their number-one draft pick.

Baker was once approached by Von Hayes. The Phillies outfielder told Baker that he was unhappy with the way he was introduced because he thought each announcement varied, depending on what he had done in his last at-bat. Baker, whose voice offers a degree of excitement, but seldom varies in tone except in cases in which a player has a particularly melodious name, was incredulous.

"I couldn't believe he actually thought that," the veteran PA announcer said. "Can you imagine anything so ridiculous?"

Mystery Guest

Broadcasting sometimes requires some quick thinking. Scott Graham put that skill to good use during the 1993 World Series.

On his pregame show, the future Phillies play-by-play man was supposed to interview someone who was standing in the dugout. One slight problem: From the press box where he stood, Graham couldn't see the dugout, and therefore didn't know the identity of the interviewee.

The director called up to give the name, and a technician sitting next to Graham wrote it down and handed it to Scott. The note said that the person Graham was about to interview was "Duke Riggiola."

"I had no clue who that was," Graham recalled. "I searched my mind, and nothing. I prayed, 'Please God, help me.'"

As the show went on the air, Graham doing his best to cover up the mystery, greeted the guest.

"Hi, Duke, what are you doing these days?" he asked.

"This is Joe Garagiola," a voice came back.

On the House

Arriving at a different city late at night is not the time to have a problem getting into a hotel room. But that's what happened to ex-Phillies pitcher-turned-broadcaster Larry Andersen upon his arrival at a hotel in Cincinnati.

It was 1:30 a.m. when Andersen was given the key to his room. When he got to the room, however, the key didn't work in the door. Returning to the front desk, Andersen was given two keys, including an extra one if the first didn't work. Neither worked.

By now, it's safe to say, Andersen was getting just a wee bit annoyed. Finally, after considerably more hassle, a hotel clerk had the bright idea to check the registration list. It said that Lawrence Andersen had checked into the room that night at 6:30 p.m. Only trouble was, it was a different Larry Andersen.

Our LA was given a key to a different room. The night manager told him that if this key didn't work, there would be beer on the house for the weekend. Alert even in the small hours of the morning, Andersen adroitly switched keys, putting one of the ones to the other room into the envelope. He then called the manager, who arrived on the scene only to find that the key that Andersen gave her didn't work.

Good move, Larry.

About the Author

Rich Westcott is a baseball writer and historian, and the author of 22 books. A veteran of more than 40 years as a writer and editor with a variety of newspapers and magazines, he is the foremost authority on Phillies history, and for 14 years was founding publisher and editor of the newspaper, *Phillies Report*. Some of Westcott's work can be seen in the historical exhibits at Citizens Bank Park. He has made frequent appearances on radio and television shows, and his byline has been seen in numerous national publications. He has also appeared in nine film documentaries, including four produced by Major League Baseball. Westcott is president of the Philadelphia Sports Writers' Association, a special advisor to the Philadelphia Sports Hall of Fame, and a member of the selection committee of the Philadelphia Baseball Wall of Fame. He has also been inducted himself into three Halls of Fame.

Other Books by Rich Westcott

The Phillies Encyclopedia (with Frank Bilovsky)
Diamond Greats – Profiles and Interviews with 65 of Baseball's History-Makers
Phillies '93 – An Incredible Season
Philadelphia's Old Ballparks
Mike Schmidt
Masters of the Diamond – Interviews with Players Who Began Their Careers More Than 50 years Ago
No-Hitters – The 225 Games, 1893-1999 (with Allen Lewis)
Splendor on the Diamond – Interviews with 35 Stars of Baseball's Past
Great Home Runs of the 20th Century
A Century of Philadelphia Sports
Winningest Pitchers – Baseball's 300-Game Winners
Tales from the Phillies Dugout
Native Sons – Philadelphia-Area Baseball Players Who Made the Big Leagues
Mickey Vernon – The Gentleman First Baseman
Veterans Stadium – Field of Memories
Phillies Essential
The Fightin' Phils – Oddities, Insights, and Untold Stories
The Mogul – Eddie Gottlieb, Philadelphia Sports Legend and Pro Basketball Pioneer

Philadelphia Phillies Past and Present
Back Again – The Story of the 2009 Phillies
Shibe Park/Connie Mack Stadium